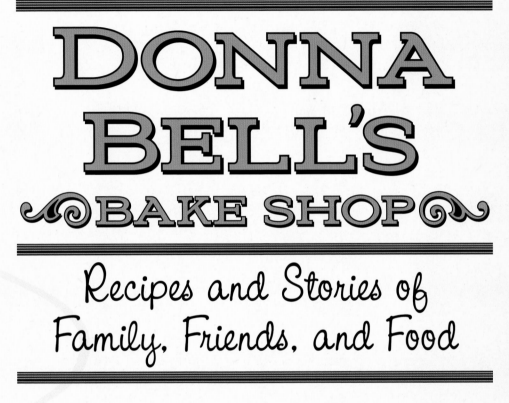

DONNA BELL'S BAKE SHOP

Recipes and Stories of Family, Friends, and Food

Pauley Perrette, Darren Greenblatt,
and Matthew Sandusky

Food and shop photographs by Ali Smith

SIMON & SCHUSTER

NEW YORK   LONDON   TORONTO   SYDNEY   NEW DELHI

Simon & Schuster
1230 Avenue of the Americas
New York, NY 10020

First Simon & Schuster hardcover edition April 2015.

SIMON & SCHUSTER and colophon are registered trademarks of Simon & Schuster, Inc.

For information about special discounts for bulk purchases, please contact Simon & Schuster
Special Sales at 1-866-506-1949 or business@simonandschuster.com.

The Simon & Schuster Speakers Bureau can bring authors to your live event.
For more information or to book an event contact the Simon & Schuster Speakers
Bureau at 1-866-248-3049 or visit our website at www.simonspeakers.com.

Interior design by Timothy Shaner, nightanddaydesign.biz
Jacket design by Jackie Seow   Jacket art by Ali Smith

Manufactured in the United States of America

10 9 8 7 6 5 4 3 2 1

Library of Congress Cataloging-in-Publication Data

Perrette, Pauley
    Donna Bell's Bake Shop : recipes and stories of family, friends, and food / Pauley Perrette,
Darren Greenblatt, Matthew Sandusky. — First Simon & Schuster hardcover edition.
       pages cm
    Summary: "The heartwarming story of how *NCIS* star Pauley Perrette and her two
best friends created a Southern-style bake shop in Manhattan—a celebration of love and
friendship with gorgeous photographs and delicious recipes." — Provided by publisher.
    1. Baking. 2. Cooking, American—Southern style. 3. Donna Bell's Bake Shop.
I. Greenblatt, Darren. II. Sandusky, Matthew. III. Title.
    TX765.P43 2015
    641.81'5--dc23   2014048249

ISBN 978-1-4767-7112-0

ISBN 978-1-4767-7118-2 (ebook)

This book is dedicated to our loved ones

Contents

Introduction 1

Part 1
Where We Come From 5

Buttermilk Biscuits 11
Cheddar Pimento Biscuits. 15
Bacon Blue Cheese Parsley Biscuits 16
Whole Wheat Biscuits 20
Blueberry-Filled Sweet Biscuits with Vanilla Sauce. 25
Apple-Filled Sweet Biscuits with Homemade Caramel Sauce . . . 26
Homemade Caramel Sauce .29
Vanilla Sauce 33
Cream Cheese Glaze 33
Lemon Glaze. 33
Orange Glaze 35
Maple Glaze 35
Apple Sausage Muffins 36
Pumpkin Chocolate Chip Loaf 41
Zucchini Walnut Bread 45
Cinnamon Almond Cranberry Coffee Cake. 46
Strawberry Scones with Lemon Glaze. 51

Part 2
A Big Idea. 53

Banana Scones with Orange Glaze 60
Cinnamon Scones with Maple Glaze 61
Dried Fruit Scones with Lemon Glaze 65
Chocolate Chip Walnut Coffee Muffins 68
Banana Pecan Muffins. 73

Contents

Part 3
Opening the Shop 75

Peach Muffin Streusel 80

Streusel Topping 81

Pumpkin Spice 81

Pineapple Cherry Crunch Muffins 82

Hummingbird Bread Pudding with Cream Cheese Glaze 87

Cranberry Orange Spice Bread Pudding with Orange Glaze. . . .90

Cheddar Jalapeño Corn Bread Squares 93

Sweet Lemon Corn Bread Muffins with Fresh Blueberries 97

Lemon Bars. 100

Shortbread Crust 102

Maple Walnut Pie Bars 105

Pumpkin Pie Bars. 108

Cheesecake Filling. 110

Frosted Brownies. 112

Oat Crust 114

Fudge Frosting. 114

Seasonal Magic Bars 117

Southern Cherry Chess Bars. 119

Fruit and Cheese Bars. 120

Contents

Part 4
Friends and Family Make It Work..... 123

Peanut Butter Bars. 126
Cranberry White Chocolate Rice Krispies Treats 130
Blueberry Cheesecake Crunch Bars. .133
Chocolate Chip Cookies 136
Turtle Cupcakes. 140
Strawberry Shortcake with Fresh Whipped Cream 143
Butter Pecan Cake with Buttercream Frosting 144
Buttercream Frosting. 146
Fresh Whipped Cream. 146
Carrot Cake with Cream Cheese Frosting. 147
Cream Cheese Frosting. 148
Champagne Cake with Strawberry Buttercream Frosting. 150
Coconut Custard Pie 154

Acknowledgments 159

Recipe Index 161

Welcome to Donna Bell's Bake Shop!

This book is the story of three friends, our journeys, and how we created a special place in honor of my mother, Donna Bell.

My mother was a lovely Southern gal with sparkling blue eyes, the sweetest smile, and a true love of Southern baking and cooking. Donna Bell was born and raised in Alabama. She first saw my dad when he drove the truck for her Tri-Hi-Y hay ride. She was twelve years old and he was seventeen. He then saw her dressed as an angel in the church Easter parade. A few years later, they met at a teenage hangout, the Sugar and Spice. He wrote her number on his friend's dusty dashboard so he could call her. It all sounds like a Southern fairy tale, but it's true. When he called her, he said, "You want to go see a flick?" At first, my mom didn't know who it was, and since they were from different sides of the Alabama tracks, she didn't know exactly what he was asking her. But she soon figured it out. It was that crazy redhead, Paul, that she'd met at the Sugar and Spice. She went to see that flick with him.

They were soon married and were together until my mom passed away from breast cancer in 2002. My sister and I are so lucky that my mom decided to go see that flick with that crazy redhead from the wrong side of the Alabama tracks.

Ever since my mother passed, my friends and family and I have been dedicated to keeping her memory alive. At the bake shop, we do this by offering customers delicious treats, and also by conveying the warmth in which she lived her life. My mom was the kindest, most sensitive person I have ever known. Her concern for the well-being of all

OPPOSITE: *Donna Bell.*

people and animals is a big part of me. And her love of baking and cooking shaped my childhood. Although we constantly moved, I have fond memories of each kitchen of my childhood. I remember my sister Andi's beautiful, long hair getting caught up in the cake beaters while we were making a cake for someone's birthday. I remember the wafting scent from the Crock-Pot, always filled with delicious chicken and noodles. I remember the smell of unleavened bread every Saturday as my mother baked the Communion for Sunday church. I always remember the kitchens.

Our bakery in the heart of Manhattan is our newest kitchen, Donna Bell's Bake Shop. It brings old charm to the big city. We'd love for you to drop in and see us sometime, but for now this book can be your way of doing that. We hope you enjoy reading the history of the bakery and have fun trying out all the recipes!

PAULEY PERRETTE
Los Angeles, 2015

Love,
Respect,
History,
and Yum!

Part 1
Where We
Come From

Growing Up

I was born in Louisiana, twenty months after my big sister, Andi. My parents, Donna and Paul, had known each other since they were teenagers in Alabama. After serving in the Air Force for years my dad was working his way up in the phone company, so our family moved often because of his job. We lived in almost every Southern state. During the rather chaotic nature of this perpetual displacement, we spent all of our vacations and holidays at a tiny lake house in the middle of the woods in Alabama. My folks had named it Pauper's Paradise. That little place became the one constant in our lives.

When we spent time at this house, all the cousins would swim in the lake, fish off the pier, climb trees, and make rope swings. And there would always be food. We would wake up to eggs, grits, biscuits, and gravy. There was something cooking all day long and then dinner would often consist of whatever fish was caught that day. My maternal grandmother, Granny Bell, had moved one cabin down so there were two kitchens going. The scents of a Southern kitchen are in every fiber of my memory. To this day, wherever I am, if I smell a ham cooking, it puts me right back in my Granny Bell's house. My sister Andi recalled these times: "From Sunday lunches, potlucks, cookouts, and holiday feasts, everyone played a part and usually had their own 'specialty' claimed as their own. Everyone willing had a job suited to their age or ability. Children stirred the sugar into the tea and hap-

Opposite: Pauley's parents, Donna Bell and Paul, on their wedding day. Above: Pauley's school photo.

7

pily volunteered to be 'taste testers.' Unsure adolescents were given well-worn, proven dishes until their confidence grew to where their suggestions for a change could be courageously voiced to the group. All steps led to that bittersweet coronation moment of preparing your first Thanksgiving turkey, with the realization that a generational scepter had been both earned and passed and your role had forever changed."

My family moved to Roswell, Georgia, which became the place we lived the longest. When you move many times as a child, you adopt coping mechanisms. My sister would lock herself in her room and read endlessly so I didn't see her much. I was an awkward kid, but friendly and funny: I was able to make people laugh. My mom and my cat were my best audience. When I was around two years old, my family found a scruffy kitten at my Aunt Daisy's farm that had been attacked by some critter and was mute. We named her Delta Dawn. I fell in love with that cat, and she became my constant companion and confidante for more than twenty years. When I was thirteen, I finally was allowed to get a dog, Tasha, and later acquired another named Jesse. I loved my pets more than anything in the world. They were my best friends. I spent my time building dams in the creek behind my house, playing with my dogs, or singing to my cat in my room.

We were very much a church family, in church at least three times a week. My dad was a deacon and elder and my mom was always baking and cooking cakes and dishes for church. My mom even baked our congregation's Communion bread. Home and church were always places to enjoy cooking, baking, and eating. To this day, no meal tastes better than a good ol' fashioned church potluck dinner. There was always the aftermath of an array of mismatched dishes with people's names written on them so you wouldn't leave with the wrong casserole pan. Cooking and baking down South were a part of every day and every experience.

I was a restless and confused teenager, like most. After graduating from high school, I enrolled in college in South Georgia. I hated being away from Delta Dawn and my dogs. I would drive home five hours each way to see them (and do my laundry). I found college to be a perfect fit for me. It was probably the most focused I have ever been in my life. I did very well in school, studying sociology, psychology, and criminal science. I graduated early and with honors. I then went back to Roswell and pursued a master's degree at Georgia State University. But that didn't last for very long, as my restlessness and curiosity led me much farther from home.

OPPOSITE TOP AND BELOW: Young Pauley with her cat, Delta Dawn. RIGHT: Pauley with her dogs, Tasha and Jesse.

Buttermilk Biscuits

Makes 10–12 biscuits

3 cups all-purpose flour

1 Tablespoon baking powder

2 teaspoons baking soda

2 teaspoons kosher salt

4 teaspoons granulated sugar

1 1/4 cups (2 1/2 sticks) cold
unsalted butter, cut into
very small pieces

1 1/2 cups buttermilk

Heat the oven to 400°F. Line a rimmed baking sheet with parchment paper. In a large bowl, combine the flour, baking powder, baking soda, salt, and sugar. Toss the cold butter pieces into the flour mixture and roughly mix with a wooden spoon, making sure not to break up or soften the butter. Pour 1 cup of the buttermilk into the flour and butter mixture, and gently stir with the wooden spoon. Stir in the remaining ½ cup buttermilk until the dough comes together. Do not overmix. With a large ice cream scooper, scoop heaping mounds of the dough onto the prepared baking sheet, gently pressing down with the scooper while releasing the dough onto the baking sheet. Bake for 7 minutes. Turn the oven temperature down to 325°F, and bake until the biscuits are golden brown, about 10 additional minutes. The melted butter in the pan will be absorbed by the biscuits as they cool. Let cool on the pan for 5 minutes and serve hot.

Growing Up

I grew up in the Philadelphia suburb of Bucks County in the '70s and '80s. During this time of aspirational luxury, my parents taught my brother and me to work hard but to also live well and be grateful for what we had. They ran their own business—a small, private high school for at-risk kids—and worked long hours, but they always made time with us kids a special priority. We often ate meals out at restaurants, so I developed a pretty sophisticated palate at a young age.

It was at home that I was fortunate to learn how to be an enterprising individual. In eighth grade, I created a clothing business. I made a silkscreen in shop class of my logo, Darren Fashions, and printed it on sweatshirts with a personalized label in the collar. My family, friends, classmates, and teachers supported my venture by purchasing these sweatshirts. I sold fifty and ended up making a good profit. This was where my industrious side began to show.

Throughout my youth, my family spent many weekends and summers at a beach house in Brigantine, New Jersey. During these trips I often helped my mom in the kitchen, getting ready for visiting friends. She made simple things that were delicious, like crab quiche, using crabs we caught in the bay behind our house.

I remember my childhood fondly. My parents truly allowed me to explore my interests, which influenced my entrepreneurial spirit and informed my love of food and my sense of entertaining guests.

RIGHT: *Darren and his family, early '80s.* BELOW: *Darren with his parents, Audrey and Irwin, New York City, 1992.*

Cheddar Pimento Biscuits

Makes 13 biscuits

3 cups all-purpose flour

1 Tablespoon baking powder

2 teaspoons baking soda

2 teaspoons kosher salt

4 teaspoons granulated sugar

1¼ cups (2½ sticks) cold unsalted butter, cut into very small pieces

2 cups shredded sharp Cheddar cheese

1 cup chopped canned pimentos, drained, then dried in a dishtowel

¼ cup finely chopped scallions

1½ cups buttermilk

Heat the oven to 400°F. Line a rimmed baking sheet with parchment paper. In a large bowl, combine the flour, baking powder, baking soda, salt, and sugar. Toss the cold butter pieces into the flour mixture and roughly mix with a wooden spoon, making sure not to break up or soften the butter. Add the cheese, pimentos, and scallions; toss again until evenly mixed. Pour 1 cup of the buttermilk into the flour and butter mixture, and gently stir with the wooden spoon. Stir in the remaining ½ cup buttermilk until the dough comes together. Do not overmix. With a large ice cream scooper, scoop heaping mounds of the dough onto the prepared baking sheet, gently pressing down with the scooper while releasing the dough onto the baking sheet. Bake for 7 minutes. Turn the oven temperature down to 325°F, and bake until the biscuits are golden brown, about 15 additional minutes. The melted butter in the pan will be absorbed by the biscuits as they cool. Let cool on the pan for 5 minutes and serve hot.

Bacon Blue Cheese Parsley Biscuits

Serves 9 or 10

Hint: The bacon in these biscuits MUST be well, well, well done—borderline on the burnt side. If not cooked properly, the bacon will end up soggy, limp, and raw-looking, with zero flavor.

3 cups all-purpose flour

1 Tablespoon baking powder

2 teaspoons baking soda

2 teaspoons kosher salt

4 teaspoons granulated sugar

1¼ cups (2½ sticks) cold unsalted butter, cut into very small pieces

2 cups (12 ounces) crumbled, very well-done (crispy) bacon

½ cup crumbled dry blue cheese or Gorgonzola

¼ cup finely chopped fresh parsley leaves

1½ cups buttermilk

Heat the oven to 400°F. Line a rimmed baking sheet with parchment paper. In a large bowl, combine the flour, baking powder, baking soda, salt, and sugar. Toss the cold butter pieces into the flour mixture and roughly mix with a wooden spoon, making sure not to break up or soften the butter. Add the bacon, blue cheese, and parsley; toss again until evenly mixed. Pour 1 cup of the buttermilk into the flour and butter mixture, and gently stir with the wooden spoon. Stir in the remaining ½ cup buttermilk until the dough comes together. Do not overmix. With a large ice cream scooper, scoop heaping mounds of the dough onto the prepared baking sheet, gently pressing down with the scooper while releasing the dough onto the baking sheet. Bake for 7 minutes. Turn the oven temperature down to 325°F, and bake until the biscuits are golden brown, about 12 additional minutes. The melted butter in the pan will be absorbed by the biscuits as they cool. Let cool on the pan for 5 minutes and serve hot.

ABOVE: *Matthew, in center front, with his brother and parents, Pittsburgh, 1970s.* LEFT: *Matthew making Christmas cookies while his brother eats them, Pittsburgh, 1981.*

Growing Up

I was raised in an old steel town along one of the three rivers out-side of Pittsburgh, Pennsylvania. As a child in the '70s and '80s, I spent most of my time dreaming of the day I would escape. Times were tough for many in the area. The steel mills were closing down and people were losing their jobs. Because of the instability in the local economy, our family lived a very modest lifestyle. All our homemade meals, delicious as they were, were frugal but imaginative. I watched how my mother could make a dinner with only a few ingredients. Leftovers were used to create new dishes—food was never wasted—and everyone in my family grew to master their own "signature" dishes over the years. I remember my mother's homemade bread, my dad's minestrone soup, my brother's cinnamon brownies (chocolate was expensive), my Aunt La's Jell-O cake, and my Aunt B's lasagna.

With all the extra care placed on preparing food and desserts, holidays were extra special occasions. This included New Year's at Aunt Terri and Uncle John's, "midwin-ter dinners" at Uncle Keith's, and Christmas at the cabin where we made decorations, ate, laughed, and chopped wood for the fireplace. My favorite time of the year was Thanksgiving, when my dad, brother, cousins, and uncles would gather in the living room to watch football games. I, on the other hand, would be found peering over my grandmother's shoulder in the kitchen asking how long to roast the turkey, or why you use flour to make gravy. By the age of ten, I started to understand some basic techniques of cooking and baking, which came in handy when my mother decided to go back to work in the early '80s. During the week, my parents would come home to a surprise homemade dinner that I had prepared all on my own. Sometimes it was only macaroni and cheese, but I felt like it was a huge accomplishment and my parents acted like it was super delicious, even though many of the times it probably wasn't.

Though my parents have often said that they wish they could have given my brother and me more when we were kids, I think my childhood prepared me with the skills I needed to leave Pittsburgh and make it on my own. I had love and support. I felt I could do anything I wanted with my life.

Whole Wheat Biscuits

Makes 9 biscuits

2 cups whole wheat flour

1 cup all-purpose flour

1 Tablespoon baking powder

2 teaspoons baking soda

1 Tablespoon kosher salt

5 teaspoons granulated sugar

1¼ cups (2½ sticks) cold unsalted butter, cut into very small pieces

1½ cups buttermilk

Heat the oven to 400°F. Line a rimmed baking sheet with parchment paper. In a large bowl, combine the whole wheat flour, all-purpose flour, baking powder, baking soda, salt, and sugar. Toss the cold butter pieces into the flour mixture and roughly mix with a wooden spoon, making sure not to break up or soften the butter. Pour 1 cup of the buttermilk into the flour and butter mixture and gently stir with the wooden spoon. Stir in the remaining ½ cup buttermilk until the dough comes together. Do not overmix. With a large ice cream scooper, scoop heaping mounds of the dough onto the prepared baking sheet, gently pressing down with the scooper while releasing the dough onto the baking sheet. Bake for 7 minutes. Turn the oven temperature down to 325°F, and bake until the biscuits are golden brown, about 10 additional minutes. The melted butter in the pan will be absorbed by the biscuits as they cool. Let cool on the pan for 5 minutes and serve hot.

Pauley Takes Manhattan

For many reasons, I felt like I had to get out of my small town and go somewhere bigger and more diverse. My cat, Delta Dawn, had died and my dog Tasha was killed in a horrible boating accident. My identity at the time was so wrapped up in my pets, I was heartbroken. I had studied New York City as a sociological model in school and was fascinated by it. I also realized there was a criminal science school there where I could finish my master's degree. I was desperate for a change, so I moved to Manhattan.

I felt very naïve as soon as I landed in the city. I had big blonde curly hair and my clothes weren't right for this stylish place. My heavy Southern accent didn't help. My father wasn't speaking to me because he didn't like this "sin city" or my new boyfriend. I felt very alone and I had no idea what I was doing. I picked up modeling jobs here and there but it was really hard to make enough money to go back to school. One day, a fellow model friend and I walked into a tiny bar and got hired as bartenders. I doubt I had actually ever made a real cocktail before in my life. I was grateful for the job and started studying bartending books with the same fervor I had in college. And that's how my bartending career began. I bartended all over the city, from the famous Bitter End on Bleecker Street to the flamboyant scenes of big New York nightclubs. I shaved my head, lost my accent, and became a super skater. I skated everywhere I went. The city and the asphalt were a part of me now.

At some point during this time, I got the news that my beloved Granny Bell had breast cancer. She was always the matriarch of the family, the one everyone looked up to, especially me. Kind and thoughtful, she was a strong woman and instilled courage in her granddaughters. After I had gone back and visited her in the hospital a few times, my parents moved Granny into their home for hospice. It had been so long since I'd gone home, I felt out of place when I visited under these already painful circumstances. Back in New York, every time I passed a deli and smelled a ham or something familiar cooking, I cried for my Granny. I missed her and my mom so much. It was always those smells of home cooking that would pull my heartstrings right back to the little kitchens in Alabama.

I was bartending in a huge club in Hell's Kitchen a few blocks from my apartment. The place was filled with all kinds of club kids in outrageously fabulous costumes. I worked twelve-hour shifts, and saved every penny. It was fast and creative and crazy. I had a white Mohawk and piercings at the time. One night, a guy—an actor—who worked in coat check came up to me and said, "I know a director who would love you." I didn't really know what that meant, but I had once overheard a girl in the bar say that she had made three thousand dollars from acting in a commercial. I really needed three thousand dollars. I found the director, walked straight into his office, and said, "Walter from coat check said you'd love me." He hired me right then and continued to employ me for many music videos, commercials, and short films.

Back at the club, one night I saw a bus boy wearing this incredible, hardcore, cable-wire jewelry. It was so cool. I asked him where he got it. He had some connection to the designer and told me he would get me some. Turns out, that encounter is how I met my best friend; the jewelry designer was Darren Greenblatt.

ABOVE: Pauley stands in front of one of her modeling advertisements.

Blueberry-Filled Sweet Biscuits with Vanilla Sauce

Makes 9 biscuits

3 cups all-purpose flour

1 Tablespoon baking powder

2 teaspoons baking soda

2 teaspoons kosher salt

⅓ cup granulated sugar

1¼ cups (2½ sticks) cold unsalted butter, cut into very small pieces

1 cup buttermilk

Nonstick cooking spray

1 cup canned blueberry pie filling

½ recipe Shortbread Crust (page 102)

Vanilla Sauce (page 33)

Heat the oven to 400°F. Line a 12-cup muffin tin with cupcake liners. Place muffin tin on a rimmed baking sheet in case any melted butter drips. In a large bowl, combine the flour, baking powder, baking soda, salt, and sugar. Toss the cold butter pieces into the flour mixture and roughly mix with a wooden spoon, making sure not to break up or soften the butter. Pour ¾ cup of the buttermilk into the flour and butter mixture and stir with the wooden spoon. Stir in the remaining ¼ cup buttermilk until the dough comes together into a ball. Use your hands if necessary. The dough will be stiff. With a large ice cream scooper, scoop the dough, scrape off excess to make an even scoop, and place in a muffin cup. Repeat to use all the dough. Spray your fingers with cooking spray. In each scoop of dough, create a well that goes almost to the bottom of the dough and is about 1½ inches in diameter. Fill each well with about 1 tablespoon blueberry pie filling. Mound the Shortbread Crust on each biscuit, pressing gently to cover the tops and seal in the blueberries. Bake for 9 minutes. Turn the oven temperature down to 325°F, and bake until the biscuits are golden

Blueberry-Filled Sweet Biscuits with Vanilla Sauce *(cont.)*

brown, about 10 additional minutes. Let cool in the tin for 5 to 10 minutes. Lift the biscuits out of the tin using a spoon. Drizzle with Vanilla Sauce and serve warm.

Apple-Filled Sweet Biscuits with Homemade Caramel Sauce

Makes 9 biscuits

3 cups all-purpose flour

1 Tablespoon baking powder

2 teaspoons baking soda

2 teaspoons kosher salt

1/3 cup granulated sugar

1¼ cups (2½ sticks) cold unsalted butter, cut into very small pieces

1 cup buttermilk

Nonstick cooking spray

1 (21-ounce) can apple pie filling

½ recipe Shortbread Crust (page 102)

Homemade Caramel Sauce (page 29)

Heat the oven to 400°F. Line a 12-cup muffin tin with cupcake liners. Place muffin tin on a rimmed baking sheet in case any melted butter drips. In a large bowl, combine the flour, baking powder, baking soda, salt, and sugar. Toss the cold butter pieces into the flour mixture and roughly mix with a wooden spoon, making sure not to break up or soften the butter. Pour ¾ cup of the buttermilk into the flour and butter mixture, and stir with the wooden spoon. Stir in the remaining ¼ cup buttermilk until the dough comes together into a ball. Use your hands if necessary. The dough will be stiff. With a large ice cream scooper, scoop the dough, scrape off excess to make an even scoop, and place in a muffin tin. Repeat to use all the dough. Spray your fingers

Apple-Filled Sweet Biscuits with Homemade Caramel Sauce *(cont.)*

with cooking spray. In each scoop of dough, create a well that goes almost to the bottom and is about 1½ inches in diameter. Fill each well with about 2 tablespoons apple pie filling. Mound the Shortbread Crust on each biscuit, pressing gently to cover the tops and seal in the apples. Bake for 9 minutes. Turn the oven temperature down to 325°F, and bake until the biscuits are golden brown, about 10 additional minutes. Let cool in the tin for 5 to 10 minutes. Lift the biscuits out of the tin using a spoon. Drizzle with Homemade Caramel Sauce and serve warm.

Homemade Caramel Sauce

1/2 cup (1 stick) unsalted butter

1/4 cup packed dark brown sugar

1 Tablespoon granulated sugar

2 Tablespoons heavy whipping cream

1 Tablespoon honey

1/4 cup sweetened condensed milk

1 teaspoon vanilla extract

Place the butter, brown sugar, granulated sugar, cream, honey, and condensed milk, in a pot. Bring to a boil over high heat. Boil, stirring continually, until smooth, for 1 to 2 minutes. Remove the pot from the heat and stir in the vanilla. Let cool in the pot for 2 to 3 minutes. Stir again, and pour the warm sauce over the dessert.

ABOVE: *Darren and Pauley, the evening before Pauley moved from New York to Los Angeles, 1996.*
LEFT: *Pauley and Darren, New York Fashion Week, 1995.*

Darren Meets Pauley

In the mid '90s, when I was in my early twenties, I started my own company designing the industrial jewelry that would eventually lead Pauley to me. I was walking home from the garment district when a fierce blond girl on Rollerblades stopped me and said, "Love your bracelet. I keep seeing people wearing your jewelry! Where can I get one?" I told her that my company created them and that I'd be happy to show her the collection. I asked her if she'd like to take a look now, while pointing up to the building behind me. Pauley looked shocked and said, "What? You live here? I live right there," directing my gaze across the street. I gave Pauley some jewelry and we exchanged numbers.

A few weeks after we met I was approached by *Women's Wear Daily,* who wanted to do a profile of my company. This was a huge opportunity, especially for a young designer. They wanted to visit our factory in New Hope, Pennsylvania, for a photo shoot. I immediately knew I wanted to use Pauley to model for the shoot. When I asked, she said yes. We spent many hours on the train ride to the shoot talking about everything: our hopes, dreams, and idiosyncrasies. By the time we arrived, I felt like I had found my long-lost sister. After the shoot we were inseparable and talked many times each day.

Pauley was welcomed into my family immediately. She had met my brother and my parents at the shoot, and then she started seeing them on their monthly weekend visits to New York City. My mom and dad's generosity and nonjudgmental qualities fostered a deep bond with her, and many of my other friends. Even with Pauley's shaved head or green Mohawk or my long hair, they would say we looked great and encouraged our creativity.

My mom got to know Donna and they shared a special moment during an exchange of letters about the budding friendship between Pauley and me. Donna called us "the amazing friends" and asked my mother, "Aren't we the luckiest that those two found each other?" I know how rare our friendship is and I am supremely grateful for what Pauley and I have.

Vanilla Sauce

2 Tablespoons unsalted butter

1½ cups sifted confectioners' sugar

½ teaspoon ground nutmeg

1 teaspoon kosher salt

2 Tablespoons whole milk

2 Tablespoons heavy whipping cream

1 teaspoon vanilla extract

Melt the butter in a small saucepan over low heat or in a glass bowl in the microwave. Let cool. In a large bowl, stir together the sugar, nutmeg, and salt. In a small bowl, whisk together the cooled melted butter, milk, cream, and vanilla. Whisk the butter mixture into the sugar until smooth.

Cream Cheese Glaze

4 ounces cream cheese, softened

3 Tablespoons sifted confectioners' sugar

¼ cup whole milk

¼ teaspoon vanilla extract

In a large bowl, whip the softened cream cheese with a spoon or hand mixer until smooth. Slowly add the sugar and beat until smooth. Mix in the milk and vanilla, and beat again with the spoon until smooth.

Lemon Glaze

2 cups sifted confectioners' sugar

5 Tablespoons fresh lemon juice

In a bowl, whisk together the sugar and lemon juice until smooth.

Matthew Meets Pauley

I didn't know anyone in Los Angeles but I was drawn to it and decided to move there in the late '90s. It was raining when I arrived at Union Station in downtown L.A., so I hopped into a taxi and told the driver to take me to Hollywood. He kept asking me for more specific instructions, but I had no idea where exactly I wanted to go so I just told him to keep driving around. As the meter in the cab racked up the fine, I panicked and asked to be let out. I looked up and saw I was standing on the corner of Hollywood and Vine—the heart of Hollywood. I walked into the first motel I saw and even though it was dirty and dangerous, I knew I only could move forward, so I quickly called it home. There was no going back.

Eventually I met a few people who needed a roommate at an artist complex on Melrose Avenue. Los Angeles was just what I was looking for at the time. It was cheap, inspiring, and the weather was incredible.

Within the first year of living in my new city, I was asked to host a television show about L.A. nightlife that a friend was producing for E! Entertainment Television. Everyone involved in this show was colorful and talented. Though I felt I had fearlessly made my way in this new city, on the outside I'm sure I appeared rather tame compared to the characters in the club scene, including the very tall, blonde, beautiful, and innocently outrageous Pauley Perrette. Out of all those large personalities, she was the most kind and genuine. We clicked instantly and before I knew it we were on our way to becoming great friends. She gave me the nickname Uncle Matthew because I would watch everyone's pets when they left town. At the time, none of our friends had any children, so my nieces and nephews were my friends' dogs and cats.

Pauley and I have been through a lot together over our seventeen-year friendship. I was there when she bought her first house, when she adopted her first rescue dog, and when she heard the news that she had gotten the part in *NCIS*. I remember one moment that showed how truly caring Pauley is. When I moved down the street from her house in the Hollywood Hills, she brought me homemade chicken and dumpling soup as a housewarming gift. It was something I would have done for a friend and I knew that I had met someone special in the sea of people in Los Angeles. Our friendship was always pretty effortless, and Pauley became part of what I called my "California family."

Orange Glaze

2 cups sifted confectioners' sugar
5 Tablespoons fresh orange juice

In a bowl, whisk together the sugar and orange juice until smooth.

Maple Glaze

2 cups sifted confectioners' sugar
9 Tablespoons real maple syrup

In a bowl, whisk together the sugar and maple syrup until smooth.

LEFT: *Matthew flying back to visit Pittsburgh from Los Angeles, 1999.* ABOVE: *After-party at Matthew's house in Hollywood, 1999, the year he and Pauley became good friends.* RIGHT: *Thanksgiving at Matthew's house in Los Angeles, 2001.*

Apple Sausage Muffins

Makes 12 muffins

2 large Granny Smith apples, peeled and cored

2 cups all-purpose flour

1½ teaspoons baking powder

1 teaspoon baking soda

2 teaspoons kosher salt

2 teaspoons granulated sugar

¾ cup (1½ sticks) cold unsalted butter, cut into very small pieces

1½ cups cooked, drained, and crumbled Italian sweet sausage

½ cup buttermilk

¼ cup sour cream

Heat the oven to 375°F. Line a 12-cup muffin tin with cupcake liners. Slice one of the apples into 12 wedges and set aside. Chop the second apple. In a large bowl, stir together the flour, baking powder, baking soda, salt, and sugar. Add the cold butter pieces and quickly press between your fingertips to break up the butter and incorporate it into the flour until the mixture resembles coarse crumbs. Add the chopped apple and sausage. In another bowl, whisk together the buttermilk and sour cream. Pour the wet ingredients into the dry and gently fold until just combined. Do not overmix; the batter should be lumpy. Using a large ice cream scooper, fill the prepared muffin cups with the batter. Top each muffin with 1 apple wedge. Bake for 7 minutes. Turn the oven temperature down to 325°F, and bake until the muffins are golden brown and firm to the touch, an additional 8 to 10 minutes. Let cool in the tin for 5 minutes. Transfer to a wire rack. Serve warm or allow to cool completely.

Pauley in Hollywood

As soon as I started appearing in commercials, music videos, and short films in New York, my new career moved very quickly. I kept booking more and more jobs and soon quit bartending. One of the commercials I did became really huge and because of it, I got an invitation to Los Angeles for what was called "pilot season." I remember thinking, "I have *no* interest in flying planes." I eventually learned that pilot season was the time when they cast actors for the new television season.

I flew to L.A. for the weekend and was cast in a TV show that shot in Phoenix, Arizona. I also got a record deal and the lead in a film. I rented a tiny apartment for four hundred twenty-five dollars in Hollywood, which had only a sleeping bag, an oil lamp, and a pillow and no electricity. I desperately missed Darren and his parents, the Greenblatts (my "Jewish family"), who had really been there for me in New York. Then I opened up the back door to my tiny apartment and saw a glowing sign that read Greenblatt's Deli. I couldn't believe it. I knew I would be OK.

I then called my friend Sean, whom I had done commercials with in New York City, and said, "Hey, could you pack up all my stuff and drive it to L.A.?" He kindly said yes and then ended up moving into the same apartment complex.

I continued to book jobs in Los Angeles and, in spite of my initial reluctance, I began to feel at home and appreciate the weather. I was working and saving my money, adjusting to my new West Coast life as an actor. Slowly, I was beginning to try to figure out who I was and where I was going. I made a big move and rented a little house. I remember the day I bought my first washer and dryer. It was amazing to me that I could clean my clothes with my own washer and dryer. I was super proud of myself. A boyfriend of mine told me about a cat that was in trouble, and I took him in. That was a huge step for me since I had refused to have another pet after my lost loves. I named this big, beautiful silver cat Kazan. He became the center of my universe. I lived there in that house for years; me, my cat, and the many strays—people and animals—who came and went.

When I wasn't on set, I spent my time with a fabulous group of creative people in a scene full of drag queens, artists, and flamboyant characters. We would throw huge events where people planned their costumes and outfits for months. In Los Angeles, I didn't have to bartend, so I would get dressed up like everyone else and have a blast. It was rock-and-roll and crazy fashion. A TV network wanted to do a documentary about all of our shenanigans. That event is how I met my other best friend, Matthew Sandusky. He was handsome and hilarious and we quickly became inseparable.

OPPOSITE: *Matthew, Pauley, and Tony in Los Angeles.*

Pumpkin Chocolate Chip Loaf

Serves 8

Nonstick cooking spray

½ cup (1 stick) unsalted butter

2 cups all-purpose flour

1 teaspoon baking powder

1 teaspoon baking soda

1 teaspoon Pumpkin Spice
  (page 81)

½ teaspoon kosher salt

1 cup semisweet chocolate chips

2 large eggs

1 cup granulated sugar

1 Tablespoon vanilla extract

½ cup canned pumpkin puree
  (not pumpkin pie filling)

½ cup sour cream

1 teaspoon dark molasses

Heat the oven to 350°F. Spray a standard 9-by-5-inch loaf pan with cooking spray. Melt the butter in a small saucepan over low heat or in a glass bowl in the microwave. Let cool. In a bowl, stir together the flour, baking powder, baking soda, Pumpkin Spice, salt, and chocolate chips. Whisk the eggs and sugar together in another bowl. Then whisk in the cooled melted butter. Add the vanilla, pumpkin puree, sour cream, and molasses; whisk until combined and smooth. Pour the wet ingredients into the dry and gently fold until just combined. Do not overmix; the batter should be lumpy. Pour the batter into the prepared loaf pan and smooth the top. Bake until a knife inserted in the center comes out clean, 50 to 60 minutes. Remove the pan from the oven and wrap it completely in foil for ½ hour. Remove the foil, take the loaf out of the pan, and transfer to a wire rack. Let cool completely before cutting.

Spending Time with Donna Bell and Pauley's Family

Over the past twenty years I have been fortunate to have spent a good amount of time with Pauley's family in the South. Pauley's mother, Donna, was beautiful and so kind to me from the minute we first met at their lake house in Alabama. She was gracious and funny and I felt an instant connection. I was also excited to be in Alabama because of the food—I was obsessed with Southern cooking and couldn't wait to help Donna in the kitchen.

During these quick trips, we would sit around the kitchen table talking, all day, every day. We would listen to Pauley's parents share stories of how they met and the romance that followed, of the twisters that tore down parts of their home. They told me about the town's history and old family tales. It all sounded so whimsical. There was something in Donna's lovely voice and Southern accent that would make reading the newspaper aloud sound like poetry.

Twenty years later, there are still so many visceral memories from those trips: Waking up to the smell of strong coffee and a good ol' Southern breakfast of scrambled eggs, coffee cakes, sweet loaves, and biscuits and gravy. Going for long walks or drives while listening to Dolly Parton tapes. Lazy afternoons telling more stories over sweet sun tea and a "li'l sweet plate," which is Southern-speak for a plate with various desserts and sweets like brownies, cookies, and nut brittles. As the sun goes down, having dinner, then retiring to the back porch to sit on rocking chairs and stare out at the moon on the lake.

I was honored that some of Donna's recipes were given to me after she passed. Those recipes and handwritten notes were a huge inspiration for us at the shop.

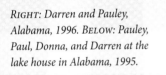

RIGHT: Darren and Pauley, Alabama, 1996. BELOW: Pauley, Paul, Donna, and Darren at the lake house in Alabama, 1995.

Zucchini Walnut Bread

Serves 8

Nonstick cooking spray

1/2 cup (1 stick) unsalted butter

1 cup shredded zucchini

2 cups all-purpose flour

1 teaspoon baking powder

1 teaspoon baking soda

1 teaspoon ground cinnamon

1/2 teaspoon kosher salt

1 cup finely chopped walnuts

2 large eggs

1 cup granulated sugar

1 Tablespoon vanilla extract

1 cup sour cream

Heat the oven to 350°F. Spray a standard 9-by-5-inch loaf pan with cooking spray. Melt the butter in a small saucepan over low heat or in a glass bowl in the microwave. Let cool. Place the zucchini on a clean dishtowel. Fold the towel around the zucchini and squeeze out as much water as you can. Make sure the zucchini is as dry as possible. Stir together the flour, baking powder, baking soda, cinnamon, salt, zucchini, and walnuts in a large bowl. Whisk the eggs and sugar together in another bowl. Whisk in the cooled melted butter. Add the vanilla and sour cream; whisk until combined and smooth. Pour the wet ingredients into the dry and gently fold until just combined. Do not overmix; the batter should be lumpy. Pour the batter into the prepared loaf pan and smooth the top. Bake until a knife inserted in the center comes out clean, 50 to 60 minutes. Cool in the pan for 5 minutes. Remove from the pan, transfer to a wire rack, and cool completely before cutting.

Cinnamon Almond Cranberry Coffee Cake

Serves 12

Nonstick cooking spray

3/4 cup (1½ sticks) unsalted butter

3 cups all-purpose flour

1½ teaspoons baking powder

1½ teaspoons baking soda

2 teaspoons ground cinnamon

1 teaspoon kosher salt

1 cup sliced almonds

1 cup dried cranberries

3 large eggs

1½ cups granulated sugar

1½ cups sour cream

1 Tablespoon vanilla extract

1 Tablespoon almond extract

Streusel Topping (page 81)

Confectioners' sugar, for dusting

Heat the oven to 350°F. Line a 9-by-13-inch baking pan with aluminum foil, allowing enough foil to overlap the edges. Spray the foil with cooking spray. Melt the butter in a small saucepan over low heat or in a glass bowl in the microwave. Let cool. Stir the flour, baking powder, baking soda, cinnamon, salt, almonds, and cranberries together in a large bowl. Whisk the eggs and granulated sugar together in another bowl. Then whisk in the cooled melted butter. Add the sour cream and vanilla and almond extracts; whisk until combined and smooth. Pour the wet ingredients into the dry, and gently fold until just combined. Do not overmix; the batter should be lumpy. Pour the batter into the prepared pan, smooth the top, and cover it evenly with Streusel Topping. Bake until a knife inserted in the center comes out clean, 40 to 50 minutes. Cool in the pan for 10 minutes. Use a sifter to dust the top with confectioners' sugar. Grab the foil handles with both hands, and lift the cake out of the baking pan. Cut into 12 squares. Serve immediately.

Birthday Cake Disaster

I have always found that food makes some of the best gifts. Every Sunday evening was "family dinner," when I cooked for my roommates, and I baked cakes as gifts for all of my friends' birthdays and weddings. For my friends in Los Angeles who had nowhere to go, I hosted giant Thanksgiving dinners each year. This was a special, and affordable, way for me to show my love.

At one point in time, pre-*NCIS* days, Pauley was leading a punk rock band called Lo-Ball and they were performing at clubs all over Hollywood. One March night, her birthday, she was playing a gig at one of our favorite hangouts. As usual, I made a big cake to surprise her, but my taxi got into an accident just as it pulled up to the club. Nobody was hurt, but the cake ended up in my chest. Luckily the club's doorman was a friend of mine and he snuck me in through the back door and into the club's office, so the line out front didn't see me covered in frosting. Pauley walked in at the same time. As I sat there, ready to cry, with this crumbled sweet disaster all over me, Pauley scooped out a giant piece of cake with her bare hand and took a huge bite. "That's the best-tasting cake I ever had in my entire life. You all have to try this," she said. For those of us who are close to her, we call things like this "typical Pauley." It's what makes her unique, loved, and special.

ABOVE: *Matthew and Pauley, December 31, 2002.*

Holidays at Home

While living in New York and Los Angeles, I would go back down South for holidays. My folks were still in Georgia until my dad retired and they moved permanently to the little lake house in Alabama. They lived in their own kind of Eden, deep in the woods. Visits would be about cooking, eating, and talking. My mom and my sister Andi were fantastic cooks and could make and bake anything. If anyone dropped by to say hello, they were usually carrying a dish of their own and would add it to whatever was on the table. Coffee was always brewing in the morning and sweet tea flowed freely all day. There was always someone in the kitchen. They would send me back to New York or Los Angeles with pound cakes and cookies. Darren visited down South with me. He is fond of everything Southern and fell in love with my mom. He was amazed at all the cooking and baking going on all the time. He loved hearing all the stories and tales everyone sits around and tells until falling asleep in their chairs. Darren embraced every aspect of my family's very Southern nature.

RIGHT: *Pauley's parents.*

Strawberry Scones with Lemon Glaze

Makes 16 scones

4 cups all-purpose flour

1 cup granulated sugar

1 Tablespoon baking powder

½ teaspoon baking soda

1 cup (2 sticks) cold unsalted butter, cut into very small pieces

12 strawberries, rinsed then dried in a dishtowel, sliced

¾ cup whole milk

½ cup heavy whipping cream

½ cup sour cream

2 teaspoons vanilla extract

1 cup strawberry preserves

Lemon Glaze (page 33)

In a large bowl, whisk together the flour, granulated sugar, baking powder, and baking soda. Add the cold butter pieces and quickly press between your fingertips to break up the butter and incorporate it into the flour until the mixture resembles coarse crumbs. Mix in the strawberries. Place the milk, heavy cream, sour cream, and vanilla extract in another bowl. Whisk together until the sour cream is fully incorporated and the mixture is smooth. Make a well in the flour mixture and pour in all the liquid. Mix with a wooden spoon until the dough comes together. Do not overmix. Cover the bowl with plastic wrap and refrigerate for 2 hours. Heat the oven to 400°F. Line two baking sheets with parchment paper. Lightly flour a work surface and place the dough on it. Cut the dough into two equal pieces. Wrap one piece in plastic wrap, and set aside in the refrigerator. Press one piece of dough down with your fingertips to flatten to an 8-inch circle, about ½ inch thick. Cut the circle into 8 equal wedges and place on a baking sheet about ½ inch apart. Bake until the scones are golden brown, 15 to 18 minutes. Let cool for 5 minutes, spread 1 tablespoon strawberry preserves on each scone. Drizzle ½ of the Lemon Glaze evenly on top. Serve warm. Repeat with the remaining piece of dough, ½ cup strawberry preserves, and remaining Lemon Glaze.

Part 2
A Big
Idea

Mom

One day, I was at home and my fax machine rang. It was from my mother. The fax read, "I have breast cancer." I guess it was easier than telling me on the phone. I was devastated. We had already gone through the excruciating pain of watching my Granny lose her battle with breast cancer a few years before, and now it had struck my mom. My mother was so young, so beautiful, and so healthy. It was a shock. She soon began chemo and radiation treatments and underwent some surgeries. We felt very hopeful at first. I would go to Alabama and she seemed to be getting healthier and stronger. I was in an all-girl punk band at the time and felt confident enough in my mom's recovery to go on tour. I then began shooting a television show in Vancouver, Canada.

Eventually, my job in Vancouver ended and I was back working in Los Angeles. I had moved from my rental house into a little Southern Colonial home I had bought that reminded me of the East Coast. I adopted two little rescue dogs, Li'l Joe, a sweet, short corgi mix, and Cece, a terrier mix that had brain damage. My pets had my heart. My life was about my critters and my acting jobs.

I was on set shooting a television show when I got a call from my dad. He told me that the doctors had found cancer all over Mom's body when she went in for a precautionary procedure. The cancer was now in her ovaries and metastasized to her lymph nodes and bones. We were shooting a scene where my character was supposed to be crying. I walked back to set ashen-faced and in shock. My director asked me what was wrong and I remember telling him, "I'm afraid if I start crying, I'll never, ever stop."

The next year of my life was spent going back and forth to Alabama to be with my mom.

I couldn't join a show as a regular cast member because I had to be able to go home. Darren traveled with me and we stayed in a hotel room across the street

OPPOSITE: Donna Bell's high school photo.

from the hospital with my sister and her kids. He was a lifesaver during this time. I was in a fog. I could not imagine not having my mother. As the cancer got worse, my dad moved my mom home for hospice. I would sit by her bed and watch her. She was so tiny. She had lost all her hair. She looked like a broken baby bird in a nest of sheets. Sometimes she was somewhat lucid, and sometimes she would talk to angels, Jesus, a president, or someone who had passed away. One time she woke up suddenly and said to me, "Do you remember my red fuzzy bathrobe?" "Yes," I replied. She smiled and said, "That was fun!" then went back to sleep. I still have that red fuzzy robe. My dad and I aimlessly wandered around the house, relying on sustenance from kind strangers' casseroles and hams. Now, there was no one cooking in the kitchen. No one telling stories and no laughter. It was just still, the stillness of pending loss and a fate unknown.

I had to fly back to Los Angeles for a weekend to shoot a job. Two of my friends planned on taking me to thrift stores the next morning to cheer me up, one of my favorite activities. But I had to cancel. My mother had died. I have always thought it was by design that she passed away during the two days I was away from her. Perhaps she thought it would be easier for me. I have almost no recollection of the funeral. The one thing I remember vividly was viewing her the day before. My mother was a Southern Lady. When she knew how sick she was, she began planning. She picked out a dress and a wig for her funeral. She asked me to please make her look pretty. She had picked out a certain lipstick. I went to the funeral home and did my mom's makeup in her casket. It was so peaceful. She looked beautiful. She was always just so beautiful.

I had a very hard time after my mom died. I missed her so much. I was so confused. I stopped celebrating my birthday, because she had loved my birthday. Holidays were excruciating. I spoke with Darren and my sister constantly about her and spent late nights crying. We all missed her so much.

A few years later, Darren came to me with an idea he had been thinking about for a long time. He wanted to keep Donna Bell's legacy alive by making and baking Southern food. Soon, Donna Bell's was born, and it started as a little food truck.

OPPOSITE: *Pauley in her twenties at home with her mother.*

Mixed Fruit
Scone
with Lemon Glaze
$3.00

Banana Scones with Orange Glaze

Makes 16 scones

4 cups all-purpose flour

1 cup granulated sugar

1 Tablespoon baking powder

½ teaspoon baking soda

1 cup (2 sticks) cold
    unsalted butter, cut
    into very small pieces

¾ cup whole milk

½ cup heavy whipping cream

½ cup sour cream

2 teaspoons vanilla extract

1 teaspoon banana extract
    (optional)

1 ripe banana, diced

Orange Glaze (page 35)

In a large bowl, combine the flour, sugar, baking powder, and baking soda. Add the cold butter pieces and quickly press between your fingertips to break up the butter and incorporate it into the flour until the mixture resembles coarse crumbs. Place the milk, heavy cream, sour cream, vanilla extract, and banana extract (if using) in another bowl. Whisk together until the sour cream is fully incorporated and the mixture is smooth. Make a well in the flour mixture and pour in all the liquid. Add the diced banana and mix with a wooden spoon until the dough comes together. Do not overmix. Cover the bowl with plastic wrap and refrigerate for 2 hours. Heat the oven to 400°F. Line 2 baking sheets with parchment paper. Lightly flour a work surface and place the dough on it. Cut the dough into two equal pieces. Wrap one piece in plastic wrap, and set aside in the refrigerator. Press the dough down with your fingertips and flatten to an 8-inch circle, about ½ inch thick. Cut the circle into 8 equal wedges and place them on one of the prepared baking sheets about ½ inch apart. Bake the scones until golden brown, 15 to 18 minutes. Let cool for 5 minutes, and drizzle with ½ of the Orange Glaze. Serve warm. Repeat with remaining piece of dough and remaining Orange Glaze.

Cinnamon Scones with Maple Glaze

Makes 16 scones

4 cups all-purpose flour

1 cup granulated sugar

1 Tablespoon baking powder

½ teaspoon baking soda

3 Tablespoons ground
cinnamon, divided

1 cup (2 sticks) cold
unsalted butter, cut
into very small pieces

¾ cup whole milk

½ cup heavy whipping cream

½ cup sour cream

2 teaspoons vanilla extract

Maple Glaze (page 35)

In a large bowl, combine the flour, sugar, baking powder, baking soda, and 2 tablespoons of the cinnamon. Add the cold butter pieces and quickly press between your fingertips to break up the butter and incorporate it into the flour until the mixture resembles coarse crumbs. Place the milk, heavy cream, sour cream, and vanilla in another bowl. Whisk together until the sour cream is fully incorporated and the mixture is smooth. Make a well in the flour mixture and pour in all the liquid. Mix with a wooden spoon until the dough comes together. Do not overmix. Cover the bowl with plastic wrap and refrigerate for 2 hours. Heat the oven to 400°F. Line 2 baking sheets with parchment paper. Lightly flour a work surface and place the dough on it. Cut the dough into two equal pieces. Wrap one piece in plastic wrap, and set aside in the refrigerator. Press the dough down with your fingertips to flatten to an 8-inch circle, about ½ inch thick. Sprinkle with 1½ teaspoons of the reserved cinnamon. Cut the circle into 8 equal wedges and place them on one of the prepared baking sheets, about ½ inch apart. Bake until golden brown, 15 to 18 minutes. Let cool for 5 minutes, then frost with ½ of the Maple Glaze. Serve warm. Repeat with the remaining piece of dough, 1½ teaspoons cinnamon, and remaining Maple Glaze.

Food-Truck Dreams of a Brick-and-Mortar Shop

In 2009, I had what I termed "fashion fatigue." After a fantastic twenty-year career in a turbulent industry, it was time for a change. I had received coverage in *Vogue*'s esteemed September issue, as well as in almost every major fashion and style magazine. I had also spoken about fashion and style on CNN, the *Today* show, and *The View*. Despite plenty of rich experiences, I craved consistency and routine, and wanted off the fashion treadmill. My brainy, handsome long-term boyfriend, Sam, and I had spent a year discussing parenthood with a single friend who was eager to have a baby with us. After taking time to work through the idea, and reconcile the pros and cons, and when our family and Pauley gave their blessings, we decided to go for it and co-parent (or, really, tri-parent) with her. Once our baby's mother was pregnant, we knew we would be spending that summer at the New Jersey Shore to be with our beautiful daughter. Olive Sophia was born in June.

The timing was perfect: Sam was a teacher and had the summer off so he could help me try a new business while we both spent the summer with our new baby. I had been fascinated by the food trucks that were gaining steam all over the country. I bought a vintage 1970s food truck for $1,250. Sam painted the outside and my brother tuned up the mechanics and built the kitchen inside. A true family affair, we named the truck Steel Magnolia.

The idea was to sell Southern desserts from the truck at a beach town. Pauley was supportive and happy that I named the business Donna Bell's, after her mother, whose recipes inspired me. I kept the menu simple and produced just enough for each day. Soon I was making and selling cupcakes and banana pudding in Asbury Park, New Jersey. By the end of that summer, as my baked goods were selling out daily, I dreamt of having a brick-and-mortar shop in New York City. Pauley wanted to get involved, but neither of us had ever run a retail storefront before. We were missing one key component: the person who knew all about the food business. Pauley mentioned that our friend Matthew might be ready for a big life change. It seemed he was interested in this industry, but would he really leave L.A. to open a shop with us in New York City?

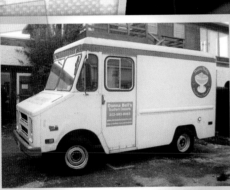

Top: *Sam, Darren, and Olive, winter 2010.* Above: *"Steel Magnolia," Jersey Shore, 2009.* Right: *Pauley meeting her goddaughter Olive with Darren and Sam, summer 2009.*

All on Board

I was in New York doing a charity runway show. A magazine had asked me several times to fly to Paris and shoot a cover, but I had declined the offer each time because I don't like to travel and it is very hard for me to be away from my pets. One night, I was sitting in a bar with Darren and his boyfriend, Sam, whom I adore, when the magazine called again. Jokingly, I said, "OK, I'll go. But Darren has to come as my handler/stylist and Sam (who speaks fluent French) has to come as my translator." To my shock, they said, "No problem."

During our trip, Darren and I talked about turning Donna Bell's food truck into Donna Bell's Bake Shop. In addition to this being a whole new undertaking as business owners, the thought of having a Southern bakery dedicated to the memory of my mother, right in the middle of Manhattan, warmed my heart. This is where Darren and I had met years ago and it almost felt like we were bringing her here as well. I talked it over with my sister and my Aunt Vicki (Donna's little sister), who were both very close to my mom. There is no way that I could have survived her passing without the support of these strong women in my life.

Darren and I often spoke about Matthew when talking about Donna Bell's. Matthew is the best baker and food creator we had ever known. He is so talented and passionate about food.

In our Los Angeles community, Matthew quickly became famous for his prowess in the kitchen. He would cook huge feasts, especially every Thanksgiving. His house, packed with people, smelled of the turkey and bread and all the other delicious food Matthew had spent days preparing. It became a very important tradition for all of us crazy kids in Los Angeles. His ability to cook delicious meals for so many people in his tiny kitchen was truly amazing. It reminded me of everyone eating and telling stories at home. And his cake baking was legendary. He didn't just bake a cake; he created a work of art. For weddings, birthdays, and other occasions, there would be a cake more beautiful than anything any of us had ever seen.

He had just finished his political science degree in Los Angeles and had extensive experience running restaurants. It became very clear that if we wanted to transform Donna Bell's from a food truck to a bake shop, the Matthew Factor would be the magic ingredient.

Dried Fruit Scones with Lemon Glaze

Makes 16 scones

4 cups all-purpose flour

1 cup granulated sugar

1 Tablespoon baking powder

½ teaspoon baking soda

1 cup (2 sticks) cold unsalted butter, cut into very small pieces

½ cup raisins

½ cup dried cranberries

½ cup chopped dried apricots

½ cup chopped dried dates

¾ cup whole milk

½ cup heavy whipping cream

½ cup sour cream

2 teaspoons vanilla extract

Lemon Glaze (page 33)

In a large bowl, combine the flour, sugar, baking powder, and baking soda. Add the cold butter pieces and quickly press between your fingertips to break up the butter and incorporate it into the flour until the mixture resembles coarse crumbs. Mix in the raisins, cranberries, apricots, and dates. Place the milk, heavy cream, sour cream, and vanilla extract in another bowl. Whisk together until the sour cream is fully incorporated and the mixture is smooth. Make a well in the flour mixture and pour in all the liquid. Mix with a wooden spoon until the dough comes together. Do not overmix. Cover the bowl with plastic wrap and refrigerate for 2 hours. Heat the oven to 400°F. Line two baking sheets with parchment paper. Lightly flour a work surface and place the dough on it. Cut the dough into two equal pieces. Wrap one piece in plastic wrap, and set aside in the refrigerator. Press the dough down with your fingertips to flatten to an 8-inch circle, about ½ inch thick. Cut the circle into 8 equal wedges, and place on a prepared baking sheet about ½ inch apart. Bake until golden brown, 15 to 18 minutes. Let cool for 5 minutes, then drizzle with ½ of the Lemon Glaze. Repeat with the remaining piece of dough and remaining Lemon Glaze. Serve warm.

Making the Big Move (Again)

By 2010, I had been living in Los Angeles for over ten years and it truly felt like home. I had been working steadily in restaurants over the years, and had held every kind of job in the industry, from waiting tables and bartending to management. I also maintained work as a production manager on small films and director reels, which was enjoyable and incredibly lucrative, but it definitely wasn't something I wanted to pursue any further. I finally went back to college and got my degree in political science after three years at Cal State L.A. Now I was getting ready to attend UCLA for my master's degree.

It was then that I received a call from Pauley. She told me that, because of my background in food, Darren wanted me to become his business partner and move to New York City. I literally thought everyone was crazy. I reflected on my situation in Los Angeles and how I didn't want to start all over again on the East Coast. I told Pauley no, and she said we would get together and talk about it again soon.

The next day, to take my mind off things, I turned on the television and came upon a show that was produced in my hometown of Pittsburgh called *Sandwiches That You Will Like.* The host, the awesome Rick Sebak, traveled around the country, interviewing restaurant owners while showcasing their signature sandwiches. As I saw business owner after business owner happily describe what they did each day, I realized I could be like them. This seemed like a sign, that something in the universe was telling me to do this. I had been fine-tuning these skills in the food industry for so long; it was now time to step it up and move into a new position. In less than twenty-four hours I was back on the phone with Pauley telling her to sign me up for the bake shop. I had been almost certain that my spontaneous days were behind me, but two weeks later, I was getting rid of most of my belongings and driving across the country to New York. So much for stability and playing it safe. Here I go again.

The Perfect Place

Darren and I were certain that we wanted Donna Bell's Bake Shop to be in the New York neighborhood where our friendship began, Hell's Kitchen. After I moved to Los Angeles, I would go back and visit our same little neighborhood. Darren's parents had moved in across the street from him and his boyfriend, so when I visited it was like walking into a family setting. Before Darren and Sam had their daughter, I would stay in their guest room instead of a hotel just to be closer. Their guest room is now the happy, bright bedroom of my goddaughter, Olive. I knew Hell's Kitchen would also be a place Matthew would love. It's just the way it feels—you can walk everywhere, people know each other.

We spent months and months looking at spaces there. Everything was taken into account: size, shape, proximity to shows and other businesses we wanted to feed. Darren's background was in design, Matthew knew everything about food, and I was a real estate person.

Growing up with a family that moved all the time, every few years or sometimes less than that, we would always be searching for a new home in a new town. The smell of cardboard boxes and a fresh coat of paint is as ingrained in my sensory memory as the ham always cooking in my granny's house. Later in her life, my mom had become a real estate agent. She was perfect for it as few families had the experience of moving as much as we did. I would sometimes go with her and look at properties. Following the tradition, I had recently been buying and restoring real estate on my own. Now the task was finding a home for our bake shop. When I was back in Los Angeles, Darren and Matthew would send me photos and specs of all kinds of properties they were exploring. Looking for the right place was daunting at times, but we knew we would eventually find the perfect spot.

OPPOSITE: *(left to right) Sam, Darren, Pauley, Darren's parents, Thomas, and Matthew.*

Chocolate Chip Walnut Coffee Muffins

Makes 12 muffins

3/4 cup (1½ sticks) unsalted
  butter

2 cups all-purpose flour

3/4 cup granulated sugar

1 Tablespoon baking powder

½ teaspoon baking soda

½ teaspoon kosher salt

1 cup semisweet chocolate chips

½ cup coarsely chopped walnuts

1 Tablespoon instant coffee
  granules

3 large eggs

½ cup whole milk

¼ cup buttermilk

¼ cup sour cream

1 teaspoon vanilla extract

Melt the butter in a small saucepan over low heat or in a glass bowl in the microwave. Let cool. In a large bowl, stir together the flour, sugar, baking powder, baking soda, salt, chocolate chips, walnuts, and instant coffee. In another bowl, whisk together the melted butter, eggs, milk, buttermilk, sour cream, and vanilla. Pour the wet ingredients into the dry and gently fold until just combined. Do not overmix; the batter should be lumpy. Cover with plastic wrap and refrigerate for at least 1 hour. Heat the oven to 375°F. Line a 12-cup muffin tin with cupcake liners. Using a large ice cream scooper, fill the prepared muffin cups about three-quarters full. Bake for 7 minutes. Turn the oven temperature down to 325°F, and bake until the muffins are firm to the touch, an additional 8 to 10 minutes. Let cool in the tin for 5 minutes, and transfer to a wire rack. Serve warm or allow to cool completely.

Finding and Designing the Space

After getting Matthew on board with the shop idea, it took about six months to find the right location and negotiate the lease, and then an additional ten months to prepare for the opening. We needed to make hundreds of decisions before we could bake the first biscuit, but it all began with finding the right space. And in New York City real estate is all about location.

We knew the demographic of Hell's Kitchen well. Matthew and I walked up and down each street every week looking for vacant storefronts and would give updates to Pauley in L.A. Then one day, as I was walking by the World Wide Plaza, a site I had passed thousands of times before, I saw a "For Rent" sign in a window of a *huge* corner space on Ninth Avenue. After verifying that this space was too big for us, the realtor showed me a smaller space in the complex that had an odd layout. It was once a nail salon. You know when people encounter just what they are looking for and say that they just knew it was right? I felt that way the second I walked in.

The logistics of the space turned out to be challenging and it was hard to map out a good floor plan. It was a triangle with windows in the front *and* back, a rarity in New York City. The back of our shop faced an arcade walkway, leading to a beautiful courtyard. The large windows would be great for showcasing what we do in the shop, but they left little space for any storage or privacy. After much discussion and numerous floor plans, we eventually found a good layout for the space and signed a ten-year lease.

For the design of the shop, we drew inspiration from our childhood homes. We used vintage wallpaper, dark wood details, and pretty curtains. We wanted to create a space where people could come in and slow down and perhaps be transported to a different place, even for just a few minutes. We finally opened the doors in early May 2011 to much excitement from everyone in the neighborhood.

Banana Pecan Muffins

Makes 10 muffins

3/4 cup (1 1/2 sticks) unsalted butter

2 ripe bananas

2 cups all-purpose flour

3/4 cup granulated sugar

1 Tablespoon baking powder

1/2 teaspoon baking soda

1/2 teaspoon kosher salt

1 teaspoon ground cinnamon

1 cup coarsely chopped pecans

3 large eggs

1/2 cup whole milk

1/4 cup buttermilk

1/4 cup sour cream

1 teaspoon vanilla extract

1/4 cup turbinado sugar

Melt the butter in a small saucepan over low heat or in a glass bowl in the microwave. Let cool. Cut 1 banana into small pieces and place in a large bowl. Add the flour, granulated sugar, baking powder, baking soda, salt, cinnamon, and pecans; stir to combine. In another bowl, whisk together the melted butter, eggs, milk, buttermilk, sour cream, and vanilla. Pour the wet ingredients into the dry and gently fold until just combined. Do not overmix; the batter should be lumpy. Cover with plastic wrap and refrigerate for at least 1 hour. Heat the oven to 375°F. Line a 12-cup muffin tin with 10 cupcake liners. Using a large ice cream scooper, fill the prepared muffin cups with the batter. Slice the remaining banana into 10 equal slices. Gently press 1 banana slice onto the top of each muffin. Sprinkle the muffins evenly with the turbinado sugar. Bake for 7 minutes. Turn the oven temperature down to 325°F, and bake until the muffins are firm to the touch, an additional 8 to 10 minutes. Let cool in the tin for 5 minutes. Transfer to a wire rack. Serve warm or allow to cool completely.

Part 3
Opening
the Shop

Finding My Inner Baker

I had spent more than twenty years cooking for friends and family and felt very confident within that range of culinary creation, but before we opened the shop I remembered thinking, "This is New York City! The best of the best come here and who do I think I am trying to pull this off?" And to add further complications, the bakery was to be "Southern" and I was not from the South (though I would joke that Pittsburgh is only forty minutes away from the Mason-Dixon Line). So I called many of my friends who were either raised in the South, or were currently living there. I asked them about their favorite desserts and family recipes. Then I watched countless hours of cooking shows, read lots of books, and practiced baking day and night in my little apartment kitchen.

While the Hell's Kitchen space was being renovated, we rented a test kitchen in Spanish Harlem. It was here that I baked for the first time using electric convection ovens and oversized multiple-quart mixers, and was finally able to scale up my recipes to yield large quantities. There were many failures during those days and I found how different it was to bake using large convection-air ovens. I would burn my cupcakes, have raw centers in my biscuits, and watch as every loaf I took out of the oven fell in the center. For weeks and weeks, it was trial and error, success and failure, but as my confidence grew we found ourselves with solid recipes and a unique exciting menu.

OPPOSITE: *Matthew at the shop making a cake for our book cover.* RIGHT: *Matthew making cupcakes in the window.*

Peach Muffin Streusel

Makes 12 muffins

3 (15-ounce) cans sliced peaches, drained well, then dried in a dishtowel

3/4 cup (1 1/2 sticks) unsalted butter

3 cups all-purpose flour

1 Tablespoon baking powder

1 teaspoon baking soda

1 teaspoon kosher salt

2 1/2 teaspoons Pumpkin Spice (recipe at right)

1/2 cup packed dark brown sugar

1/2 cup granulated sugar

3 large eggs

1/2 cup whole milk

1/4 cup buttermilk

1/4 cup sour cream

1 Tablespoon vanilla extract

Streusel Topping (recipe at right)

Reserve 12 peach slices for topping the muffins. Finely dice the remaining peaches and measure out 1½ cups. Reserve the remainder for another use. Melt the butter in a small saucepan over low heat or in a glass bowl in the microwave. Let cool. In a large bowl, whisk together the flour, baking powder, baking soda, salt, and Pumpkin Spice. Whisk in both brown and granulated sugars. In a separate bowl, whisk together the melted butter, eggs, milk, buttermilk, sour cream, and vanilla. Stir in the diced peaches. Pour the wet ingredients into the dry and gently fold until just combined. Do not overmix; the batter should be lumpy. Cover with plastic wrap and refrigerate for at least 1 hour. Heat the oven to 400°F. Line a 12-cup muffin tin with cupcake liners. Using a large ice cream scooper, fill the prepared muffin cups with the batter. Cover each scoop of batter with Streusel Topping and top with 1 peach slice. Bake for 10 minutes. Turn the oven temperature down to 350°F. Bake until the muffins are firm to the touch, about 15 minutes more. Let cool for 10 minutes in the tin. Transfer to a wire rack to cool completely, or serve warm.

Streusel Topping

1 cup all-purpose flour

1½ teaspoons kosher salt

¾ cup packed dark brown
  sugar

1 Tablespoon ground cinnamon

¾ cup (1½ sticks) cold
  unsalted butter, diced

Whisk together the flour and salt in a large bowl. Whisk in the brown sugar and cinnamon. Add the cold diced butter and cut in with a pastry blender or two forks until the streusel resembles coarse meal.

Pumpkin Spice

Makes about 7 tablespoons

¼ cup ground cinnamon

4 teaspoons ground nutmeg

1 Tablespoon ground ginger

1 Tablespoon ground allspice

Mix the cinnamon, nutmeg, ginger, and allspice together in a small bowl. Store in a small container.

Pineapple Cherry Crunch Muffins

Makes 12 muffins

3/4 cup (1 1/2 sticks) unsalted butter

1 (16-ounce) jar maraschino cherries, drained

2 cups all-purpose flour

1/2 cup granulated sugar

1/4 cup packed light brown sugar

1 Tablespoon baking powder

1/2 teaspoon baking soda

1/2 teaspoon kosher salt

3 large eggs

1/4 cup whole milk

1/4 cup buttermilk

1/4 cup sour cream

1 teaspoon vanilla extract

1 cup canned crushed pineapple in juice, not drained

Streusel Topping (page 81)

Melt the butter in a small saucepan over low heat or in a glass bowl in the microwave. Let cool. Remove any stems from the cherries. Set aside 12 cherries for the topping. Chop the remaining cherries; you will have about 1 cup. In a large bowl, stir together the flour, granulated sugar, brown sugar, baking powder, baking soda, and salt. In another bowl, whisk together the melted butter, eggs, milk, buttermilk, sour cream, and vanilla. Add the pineapple and its juice and the chopped cherries. Pour the wet ingredients into the dry and gently fold until just combined. Do not overmix; the batter should be lumpy. Cover with plastic wrap and refrigerate for at least 1 hour. Heat the oven to 375°F. Line a 12-cup muffin tin with cupcake liners. Using a large ice cream scooper, fill the prepared muffin cups with the batter. Cover each scoop with Streusel Topping and top with a whole maraschino cherry. Bake for 7 minutes. Turn the oven temperature down to 325°F, and bake until the muffins are firm to the touch, an additional 10 to 12 minutes. Let cool in the tin for 5 minutes and transfer to a wire rack. Serve warm or allow to cool completely.

Felix and Oscar of the Baked-Goods World

Matthew and I spend every day together in the shop and we often joke about how we ended up working so closely together. How did Matthew, the West Coast transplant who spent ten years amidst the Hollywood club scene, and Darren, a fashion industry insider for almost twenty years, come to be comfortable at a Restaurant Depot in the Bronx at 3:00 a.m., buying four hundred pounds of flour? We constantly laugh and reflect upon how much our lives have changed.

Early one morning, when we were developing recipes in our Spanish Harlem test kitchen, we met up at a twenty-four-hour Mexican cantina to grab some breakfast. As usual, I had a bunch of questions for the waiter: Did they have black or pinto beans, corn or flour tortillas? And then I ordered huevos rancheros with guacamole and both hot and mild salsa, coffee with milk, and a side of chorizo that looked so good when it was delivered to another table. Matthew ordered scrambled eggs, plain white toast, and coffee. When the food arrived I had a huge smile, Matthew rolled his eyes eyeing my many plates, and I couldn't wait to dig in.

That breakfast illustrates the vast personal differences in tastes between Matthew and me and how we also complement each other. We're like Oscar and Felix from *The Odd Couple,* total opposites yet somehow it works. I like restaurants and Matthew likes bars; I like a plan and Matthew likes to be spontaneous. There are days when one of us is down and the other is up and offers support. Like a brotherly relationship, we can disagree but we always have each other's back. And it's great that we have a third partner in Pauley. She listens and weighs in when there's a disagreement or a big decision to make and helps us solve problems.

OPPOSITE: *Opening day and first customer.*
ABOVE: *Our annual Christmas in July tradition at the shop.*

Hummingbird Bread Pudding with Cream Cheese Glaze

Serves 8

Hint: The night before preparing this recipe, let the bread sit out to dry so it will absorb more custard when it bakes.

2 bananas

6 large eggs

1 cup granulated sugar

3 cups whole milk

2 Tablespoons vanilla extract

1 Tablespoon ground cinnamon

1 (20-ounce) can sweetened crushed pineapple, not drained

1 cup shredded sweetened coconut

1 cup chopped pecans

½ loaf French bread, cubed or torn into small pieces, and dried overnight

Nonstick cooking spray

Cream Cheese Glaze (page 33)

1 cup finely chopped or crushed pecans, toasted, for sprinkling on top

Peel the bananas. Cut each one in half lengthwise, turn, and cut in half lengthwise again. Slice crosswise to make small pieces. In a large bowl, whisk together the eggs, sugar, milk, vanilla, and cinnamon. Stir in the banana pieces, pineapple and juice, coconut, and chopped pecans. Mix in the bread. Cover with plastic wrap and refrigerate for 20 to 30 minutes. Heat the oven to 350°F. Spray a 9-by-13-inch ceramic or glass baking dish with cooking spray. Stir the mixture well, and pour it into the prepared pan. Bake until golden, 50 to 55 minutes. For safety, check that the internal temperature is 160°F to ensure eggs are cooked. Do not overbake or the bread pudding will be too dry. Let the bread pudding cool slightly, then drizzle Cream Cheese Glaze over the warm pudding. Top with the toasted pecans and serve warm. Store, covered, in the refrigerator. You can reheat it in the microwave.

ABOVE: *The owners and the crew.* BELOW: *Matthew and Kareem making pumpkin pies.* OPPOSITE: *Rodger with his first Lemon Bars.*

The Rewards of Owning a Small Business

There are many things I love about owning a business and being my own boss. I think the greatest one is the ability to offer people jobs. But the downside is that I always want to hire everyone who walks through the door. During my years prior to this venture, I worked many jobs, some excellent, some horrible. I made a promise to myself that if I were ever in a position of being in charge, I would never come close to emulating the terrible bosses I had encountered.

When hiring, I look for people who clearly have a passion for what they do. Our dishwasher, Rodger, took an interest when I was baking in the kitchen. I noticed him looking over my shoulder while I was frosting cakes and cutting scones. One day I had a million things to do so I turned to Rodger and said, "You can make this muffin batter, can't you? Sure you can." I decided to train him, and found out that there was a pastry prodigy under my nose the entire time. Because of his hard work, dedication, and natural talent, he is one of the best bakers we have ever had.

I am so proud of some of the people we have been fortunate enough to hire. I can honestly say we have a Donna Bell's family that I will always be grateful for. I look forward to seeing members of the family one day open their own shops, and I always let them know they can do anything with their lives they want to. I feel so fortunate to be in a position where I can pass down everything I've learned over the years, including all the amazing things my parents taught me when I was younger.

Cranberry Orange Spice Bread Pudding with Orange Glaze

Serves 8 to 10

Hint: The night before preparing this recipe, let the bread sit out to dry so it will absorb more custard as it bakes.

6 large eggs

2½ cups whole milk

1½ cups granulated sugar

Grated zest and juice of 1 orange

1 Tablespoon vanilla extract

3 Tablespoons Pumpkin Spice (page 81)

3 cups fresh or thawed frozen cranberries

½ loaf French bread, cubed or torn into small pieces and dried overnight

Nonstick cooking spray

Orange Glaze (page 35)

Whisk together the eggs, milk, sugar, orange zest and juice, vanilla, and Pumpkin Spice in a large bowl. Stir in the cranberries. Mix in the bread. Cover with plastic wrap and refrigerate for 20 to 30 minutes. Heat the oven to 350°F. Spray a 9-by-13-inch baking dish, preferably ceramic or glass, with cooking spray. Stir the mixture well and pour into the prepared pan. Bake until golden, 50 to 55 minutes. For safety, check that internal temperature is 160°F to ensure the eggs are cooked. Do not overbake or the bread pudding will be too dry. Let the bread pudding cool slightly, then drizzle Orange Glaze over the warm pudding. Serve warm. Store, covered, in the refrigerator. You can reheat it in the microwave.

Cheddar Jalapeño Corn Bread Squares

Makes 12 squares

Nonstick cooking spray

1/4 cup (1/2 stick) unsalted butter

2 cups all-purpose flour

1 cup plus 1 Tablespoon yellow cornmeal, divided

4 teaspoons baking powder

1 teaspoon baking soda

1 teaspoon kosher salt

4 large eggs

1/3 cup granulated sugar

3/4 cup sour cream

1/2 cup vegetable oil

1/4 cup buttermilk

1/2 cup canned creamed corn

1 cup shredded sharp Cheddar cheese

1 jalapeño pepper, ribs and seeds removed, diced

Heat the oven to 375°F. Line a 9-by-13-inch baking pan with foil, leaving 2 inches overhanging each side. Spray the foil with cooking spray. Melt the butter in a small saucepan over low heat or in a glass bowl in the microwave. Let cool. Combine the flour, 1 cup of the cornmeal, baking powder, baking soda, and salt in a large bowl. Whisk the eggs and sugar together in another bowl. Add the melted butter, sour cream, oil, buttermilk, creamed corn, Cheddar, and jalapeño. Mix to combine. Pour the wet ingredients into the dry and gently mix until combined. The batter should be lumpy. Spread the batter into the prepared baking pan. Smooth the top. Sprinkle the remaining 1 tablespoon cornmeal over the batter. Bake until a knife inserted in the center comes out clean and the corn bread is firm to the touch, 30 to 35 minutes. Cool for 5 minutes. Grab the foil handles with both hands, and lift entire corn bread out of the baking pan. Cut into 12 squares. Serve warm.

My Learning Curve

At Donna Bell's I have learned so much each day, and while it hasn't been easy, it has always been rewarding. My learning curve was the steepest out of everyone we hired. Most of our crew had been working in this industry for years, but my first day in the café business was the day we opened the doors.

As a creative entrepreneur I had always focused on the big picture, working on building brands and developing concepts. At Donna Bell's, I worked on these macro ideas in the beginning, garnering big press or expansion of the business. But I soon realized that this business is also about the small details and immediate processes that ensure spectacular food and great customer service. Some things came naturally, like dealing directly with customers and selling things that are delicious. But others did not, like remembering to turn off the coffee machines at night. Understanding the New York City rules and regulations about food and food safety were easy enough to learn on paper, but difficult to put into practice on a daily basis. I made a *huge* closing-the-shop to-do list and referred to it each night. I had another for the morning opening.

So much of the success of the day depends on how the people before you prepare for each other. Our p.m. bakers do a lot of the prep for the a.m. bakers, which helps to set up the day. Grinding at least twelve bags of coffee so the crew doesn't have to do it during the breakfast rush may seem like a small thing, but it really helps make the shift go smoothly.

Sweet Lemon Corn Bread Muffins with Fresh Blueberries

Makes 20 muffins

1/4 cup (1/2 stick) unsalted butter

2 cups fresh blueberries, stems removed

3 cups all-purpose flour

1 cup yellow cornmeal

1 Tablespoon baking powder

2 teaspoons baking soda

4 large eggs

1 1/4 cups granulated sugar

1 cup sour cream

1/2 cup vegetable oil

1/4 cup buttermilk

Grated zest and juice of 1 lemon

Lemon Glaze (page 33)

Heat the oven to 375°F. Line a 12-cup muffin tin with cupcake liners. Melt the butter in a small saucepan over low heat or in a glass bowl in the microwave. Let cool. Rinse and drain the blueberries. Gently dry them in a dishtowel. Combine the flour, cornmeal, baking powder, baking soda, and blueberries in a large bowl. Whisk together the eggs and sugar in another bowl. Add the melted butter, sour cream, oil, buttermilk, and lemon zest and juice. Pour the wet ingredients into the dry and gently mix until combined. The batter should be lumpy. With a large ice cream scooper, scoop the batter into the cups of the prepared muffin tins, filling each three-quarters full. Bake until a knife inserted in the center of a muffin comes out clean and the muffin is firm to the touch, 25 to 30 minutes. Cool for 5 minutes. Frost with Lemon Glaze. Serve warm.

Ups and Downs

Leaving my life in Los Angeles behind was very difficult. Everything happened so fast and once the dust settled I felt lonely in New York and unsure that I had made the right decision. All of my friends lived in Los Angeles and aside from a handful of acquaintances, Darren was really the only person I knew in the city. His family was very sweet and included me in many of their special occasions, such as birthday parties, Christmas, and weekends at their beach house. But I also left Pauley in Los Angeles and it was quite an adjustment not seeing her all the time. I was turning forty, and making this big move seemed a much more daunting task than when I was younger. But I eventually came to realize the benefits of living and working in New York.

One of the biggest bonuses of moving to New York City was that I was much closer to my family in Pittsburgh. Not only could I go back to Pennsylvania for a weekend by bus, they were able to come visit the city all the time. I am thrilled that my apartment is in the middle of everything so that friends can stay with me instead of a pricey hotel. In addition to these awesome perks, one day I left the shop and on my walk home I was stopped a dozen times. I heard, "Hi, Matthew" and "Hey there, Donna Bell's!" and "When are you making chocolate cake?" Suddenly I realized how nice it felt to be part of this new neighborhood. How incredibly grateful and lucky I was to have so many places that I can call home. Pittsburgh, Los Angeles, and New York. My heart belongs to all three.

OPPOSITE: Darren and Matthew's family (mom, cousin Celeste, and Aunt B) helping out at the Ninth Avenue International Food Festival, May 2013.

Lemon Bars

Makes 12 bars

Nonstick cooking spray
Shortbread Crust (page 102)
4 large eggs
2 cups granulated sugar
2/3 cup fresh lemon juice
   (4 large lemons)
1/3 cup all-purpose flour
Confectioners' sugar, for dusting

Heat the oven to 350°F. Line a 9-by-13-inch baking pan with aluminum foil, allowing enough foil to overlap the edges. Spray the foil with cooking spray. Place the Shortbread Crust into the prepared pan, making sure to distribute evenly. Press down on the crumbs to form a crust. Bake 10 minutes. When crust has been baking for 5 minutes, whisk together the eggs and sugar in a large bowl. Add the lemon juice and flour and whisk until smooth. When the crust is done, take it out of the oven. Let cool for 2 minutes. Pour the whisked custard very slowly onto the crust and spread to cover. Tent the pan with aluminum foil, making sure the foil does not touch the top of the custard. Return the bars to the oven and bake for 30 to 35 minutes. Remove the foil. If the lemon filling is still jiggly, return the pan to the oven and bake, uncovered, until firm, another 5 to 10 minutes. Cool completely in the pan. Grab the foil handles with both hands and lift the bars out of the pan. Use a sifter to dust the tops of the bars completely with confectioners' sugar, and cut into 12 bars.

Shortbread Crust

2 cups all-purpose flour

1 cup granulated sugar

1 teaspoon kosher salt

1 cup (2 sticks) cold unsalted
    butter, cut into small pieces

Place the flour, sugar, and salt in a processor fitted with the steel blade and pulse a couple of times to combine. Add the cold butter and pulse a few times until mixture resembles coarse meal. Be careful not to process too long or it will turn into a dough.

Or to make by hand, in a large bowl, whisk together the flour, sugar, and salt. Add the cold butter pieces and quickly press between your fingertips to break up the butter into the flour until the mixture resembles coarse crumbs.

Ready to Go

As our little shop came together, it quickly became apparent that people really liked the idea of getting Southern comfort food right in the middle of New York City. When I was in Los Angeles, I would tell people that we were starting a Southern bake shop in New York City and they would get really excited. We knew it was going to grow into a place that really meant something to people. After years of planning and months of preparing, our shop was finally ready. We had an opening party with all our family and friends. Many people traveled to be there. It was an enormous show of love and support from all over. The shop is so tiny that we used a space next door to accommodate all of our well-wishers. It was such a happy occasion.

In Los Angeles, I have been blessed with the best job in the world, playing Abby Sciuto on *NCIS*. Borrowing from my own life, the writers made Abby from the South. Abby bakes and cooks. Abby goes to church. Abby hugs everyone. Abby adores animals. She is a special character that fans have really embraced. Not only do I enjoy every minute of being able to portray this character, I also have the best fans.

When I announced on social media that we were opening the bake shop, the fans were very excited and supportive. I saw that this shop would be a great way for fans to connect with Abby. *NCIS* fans from all over the world have traveled to Hell's Kitchen to visit Donna Bell's. They take photos in front of the shop, take photos with Matthew and Darren, and tweet me about what tasty treats they had. It always makes me smile that my fans are partaking in a bit of history by being part of Donna Bell's.

Maple Walnut Pie Bars

Makes 24 bars

Nonstick cooking spray

Shortbread Crust (page 102)

½ cup (1 stick) unsalted butter

¼ cup packed dark brown sugar

1 Tablespoon granulated sugar

2 Tablespoons heavy whipping cream

1 Tablespoon honey

¼ cup sweetened condensed milk

½ cup real maple syrup

½ cup light corn syrup

1 teaspoon vanilla extract

6 cups walnuts

½ cup semisweet chocolate chips

⅓ cup shredded sweetened coconut

Heat the oven to 350°F. Line a 9-by-13-inch pan with aluminum foil, allowing enough foil to overlap the edges. Spray the foil with cooking spray. Place the Shortbread Crust into the prepared baking pan, making sure to distribute evenly. Press down on the crumbs to form a crust. Bake until golden brown, about 25 minutes. While the crust is baking, place the butter, brown sugar, granulated sugar, cream, honey, and condensed milk in a pot. Bring to a boil, stirring continually. Reduce heat to medium, and add the maple and corn syrups. Cook for an additional 5 minutes, stirring continually until smooth. Remove the pot from the heat, and add the vanilla and walnuts, stirring to make sure the nuts get evenly coated. Let cool in the pot for 2 to 3 minutes. Stir again just before using. When the Shortbread Crust is done, remove it from the oven, and immediately pour the walnut mixture over the crust and spread it out evenly. Sprinkle the chocolate chips and coconut evenly over the top. Cool completely in the pan. Grab the foil handles with both hands, and lift the bars out of the baking pan. Cut into 24 bars.

Daily Shop Life

Each morning we set up the counter it reminds me of the fashion industry—we present the daily offering just like a designer's new collection, with the goal that the customer will make a purchase. But I've found that it is now much easier to convince people to buy something when the choices are so abundant, delicious, and reasonably priced. When an editor asked me about my transition from fashion to bakeshop owner, I jokingly said it was "extremely rewarding to see the smiling faces of people buying a three-dollar scone versus the miserable faces of people buying a three-thousand-dollar handbag." Making people happy every day is priceless.

The day begins very early for us. We make everything in-house using fresh ingredients, purchased locally if possible, and everything is made in small batches. Matthew and the bakers arrive at 4 a.m. and, by the time I get there at 6 a.m., there are warm trays of delicious baked goods waiting to be plated. We only have one large and one small oven so the day's success is very dependent on a strategic baking schedule. By 10 a.m. most of the breakfast pastries are sold out and we put out new items. Savory lunch items, brownies, cookies, cupcakes, and cakes are displayed around noon. We have a massive wave of customers in the late afternoon, with workers stopping by to get a coffee and a treat or young mothers coming in to get dessert for the night. In the evening we have another rush of folks stopping by on their way home or Broadway actors and crew desperate for a pick-me-up before work. We're on a first-name basis with many of them. They ask about my daughter and give us wine for holidays. They will bring their mothers into the shop and share stories of how our cake takes them back to their childhood. Food is a universal connector.

I love when tourists return to the shop every day of their stay in the city. Many of Pauley's fans make the trek and end up coming back or referring their friends and relatives because of the food. A loyal fan of Pauley's comes twice a year from an island off Canada to fill an empty suitcase with treats. She orders enough baked goods to freeze and enjoy every Tuesday while watching *NCIS*. Super sweet.

Pumpkin Pie Bars

Makes 12 bars or 24 mini bars

Nonstick cooking spray

Shortbread Crust (page 102)

2 cups canned pumpkin puree
   (not pumpkin pie filling)

1 large egg

3/4 cup granulated sugar

1/4 cup sweetened condensed milk

1 Tablespoon all-purpose flour

2 teaspoons Pumpkin Spice
   (page 81)

Streusel Topping (page 81)

1/2 cup old-fashioned oats
   (not quick cooking)

Cheesecake Filling (page 110)

Heat the oven to 350°F. Line a 9-by-13-inch baking pan with aluminum foil, allowing enough foil to overlap the edges. Spray the foil with cooking spray. Place the Shortbread Crust into the prepared baking pan, making sure to distribute evenly. Press down on the crumbs to form a crust. Bake until golden brown, about 15 minutes. When the crust has been baking for 10 minutes, make the pumpkin filling: Place the pumpkin, egg, sugar, condensed milk, flour, and Pumpkin Spice in a large bowl. Whisk together until smooth. Remove the crust from the oven and immediately pour on the pumpkin filling, very slowly, then spread to cover. Bake for an additional 15 minutes. Meanwhile, combine the Streusel Topping with the oats in a large bowl. Take the pan out of the oven and spread the Cheesecake Filling carefully over the pumpkin filling. Sprinkle the oat streusel evenly on top. Return the pan to the oven and bake until golden brown, another 20 to 25 minutes. Cool completely in the pan. Refrigerate for at least 1 hour before cutting. Grab the foil handles with both hands, and lift the bars out of the baking pan. Cut into 12 or 24 bars. The bars will be soft like pumpkin pie.

Cheesecake Filling

1 pound (two 8-ounce packages)
  cream cheese, softened

3/4 cup granulated sugar

1 large egg

2 teaspoons vanilla extract

1 teaspoon fresh lemon juice

3 Tablespoons all-purpose flour

In a medium bowl, with an electric mixer on medium speed, or a large spoon, beat the cream cheese and sugar until smooth. Reduce speed to low and add the egg, vanilla, and lemon juice. Add the flour and beat for 30 seconds. Scrape the bowl and beat for another 30 seconds, until creamy and smooth.

What Did We Get Ourselves Into?

Behind the scenes, the day-to-day operations of Donna Bell's involve lots of hard work and intense sacrifice. I often work until 2 a.m. or stay up all night, and literally work seven days a week. I have even ended up in the hospital, twice, with severe back injuries. From cuts and burns, to broken refrigerators and floods, we always must stay on alert because disaster can strike at any moment. My role at the shop doesn't stop at baking cakes; there are orders to be taken, phone calls and schedules to be made, deliveries, and a million other little details that really add up. Time becomes a luxury so you must learn to manage it well if you're the owner of a bakery. Even though there are times I feel extremely overwhelmed and frustrated, I must remind myself how fortunate I am, and how wonderful this experience really is. I am grateful every day for this opportunity and the chance to pursue my dream.

Since we opened the shop, the city has endured its disasters, including two major hurricanes. We were one of the few businesses to remain open in our neighborhood during both hurricanes Irene and Sandy. We let people charge their phones in the lobby, and we donated food to the Red Cross. Our neighbors were very excited to have a place to eat and when word got out from the local hotels that we were open for business; we had lines down the block with hungry visitors. To this day we still have customers who say they "discovered" us during one of the hurricanes, and they have been coming ever since. Finding the silver linings in dark situations is what really gets you through. No matter what gets thrown our way, I wouldn't trade it for anything in the world. I absolutely, completely, love all of it.

RIGHT: *Shopping locally for all of our ingredients.*

Frosted Brownies

Makes 12 brownies

Nonstick cooking spray
Oat Crust (page 114)
1/2 cup all-purpose flour
1/4 cup unsweetened cocoa powder
1/2 teaspoon kosher salt
2 large eggs
1/2 cup granulated sugar
1/2 cup packed light brown sugar
1/2 cup (1 stick) unsalted butter
1 cup semisweet chocolate chips
Fudge Frosting (page 114)

Heat the oven to 350°F. Line a 9-by-13-inch baking pan with aluminum foil, allowing enough foil to overlap the edges. Spray the foil with cooking spray. Press the Oat Crust into the prepared baking pan. Set aside. In a large bowl, whisk together the flour, cocoa powder, and salt. In another bowl, whisk the eggs with the granulated and brown sugars until smooth. Microwave the butter for 1 minute. Add the chocolate chips and stir until fully melted. Let cool slightly. Pour the chocolate into the egg mixture, and mix well. Make a well in the flour mixture. Pour in the egg mixture and fold until fully incorporated. Pour the brownie batter onto the Oat Crust. Smooth out until even. Bake for 30 minutes. Remove from oven and start making the Fudge Frosting. Let the brownies cool for 5 minutes and frost the warm brownies with the Fudge Frosting. Cool completely in the pan. Grab the foil handles with both hands, and lift the brownies out of the baking pan. Cut into 12 squares.

Oat Crust

2 cups all-purpose flour

1½ cups old-fashioned oats
  (not quick-cooking)

1½ cups packed light brown
  sugar

2 teaspoons kosher salt

1¼ cups (2½ sticks) cold
  unsalted butter, cut into
  small pieces

Place the flour, oats, sugar, and salt in a food processor fitted with the steel blade. Pulse a couple of times to combine. Add the cold butter and pulse a few times until the mixture resembles coarse meal. Be careful not to process too long or it will turn into a dough.

Or, to make by hand, in a large bowl, whisk together the flour, oats, sugar, and salt. Add the cold butter pieces and quickly press between your fingertips to break up the butter into the flour until the mixture resembles coarse crumbs.

Fudge Frosting

¼ cup (½ stick) unsalted
  butter

⅓ cup heavy whipping cream

½ cup semisweet chocolate chips

1 teaspoon vanilla extract

¼ cup unsweetened cocoa powder

3 cups sifted confectioners' sugar

Melt the butter in a medium saucepan over low heat. Add the heavy cream and bring to a low boil. Remove from the heat and add the chocolate chips and vanilla. Whisk until fully melted. While hot, quickly add the cocoa powder and confectioners' sugar; beat with an electric mixer until smooth.

Friendship Comes First

One of the very special things about Donna Bell's is the way Matthew creates new things on the menu. In addition to the yummy treats customers can always count on, Matthew always has something nice and new to offer. For Pride Week, he made beautiful rainbow cupcakes. There will be something themed for fall, for Thanksgiving, and for anything that inspires him.

I gave up sugar for Lent and then ended up staying off it completely. That was an ironic change for me, since I own a bake shop. My sister Andi said, "When my sister first cut out sugar, I remember plaintively asking, 'How can I show you I love you if you won't let me bake for you?' and I really, desperately needed to know the answer." My sister and Matthew are very similar. They both have not only the talent, but the passion for baking anything. Whenever I go to Andi's house in Tennessee, there is always a table full of amazing creations she's been baking for a week, often assisted by my niece Lauren. They are carrying on the tradition of my mom, as does Matthew. He also didn't know how to feed me after I kicked sugar. One night I had a dream about a whole-wheat cranberry muffin. I called Matthew the next day and told him about my muffin dream. The next time I was in New York, there it was, the muffin from my dream. It was one of the most delicious things I'd ever had. Whenever I come to town, a whole-wheat muffin is usually waiting for me.

Matthew and Darren have spent years working out the day-to-day of running the shop full time. The three of us have a system of working together, fixing problems, and always remembering that friendship comes first.

RIGHT: Matthew texting Pauley a picture of her Whole Wheat Muffins.

Seasonal Magic Bars

Makes 24 bars

Nonstick cooking spray

Shortbread Crust (page 102)

1 cup Reese's Pieces

3/4 cup shredded sweetened coconut

3/4 cup chopped pecans

1/2 cup sweetened dried cranberries

1/4 cup white chocolate chips

1/4 cup semisweet chocolate chips

1/2 cup sweetened condensed milk

1/4 cup evaporated milk

Heat the oven to 350°F. Line a 9-by-13-inch pan with aluminum foil, allowing enough foil to overlap the edges. Spray the foil with cooking spray. Place the Shortbread Crust into the prepared baking pan, making sure to distribute evenly. Press down on the crumbs to form a crust. Bake until golden brown, about 25 minutes. Meanwhile, in a large bowl, mix together the Reese's Pieces, coconut, pecans, cranberries, white chocolate chips, and semisweet chocolate chips. Remove the pan from the oven and immediately spread the chips mixture over the crust. Mix the condensed milk and evaporated milk together in a small bowl or measuring cup. Drizzle evenly over the top. Bake for 10 minutes. Cool completely in the pan. Grab the foil handles with both hands, and lift the pastry out of the baking pan. Cut into 24 bars.

OPPOSITE: Southern Cherry Chess Bars (left), Seasonal Magic Bars (center), Fruit and Cheese Bars (right).

A Catering Order Story

About a year after we opened we got our biggest catering order. We usually receive orders for cakes for special occasions, or mini platters of breakfast pastries or desserts. But on this day we received a request for four thousand mini bars to be delivered to five different locations in SoHo by 10 a.m. the following week. Since our shop is small, deciding if we should take the order was a big discussion. Matthew and I went back and forth talking about how we could do it. I told Matthew I was nervous because four thousand mini bars is a *huge* amount of food to make in one night, plus the normal amount that we would need for the shop that day—and we *don't deliver*. But Matthew loves a challenge, and explaining this to him only made him more eager to take the job.

Matthew said he could handle it by himself as long as the prep was done. He wanted to keep our normal morning crew on track to prepare for the day. So alone, Matthew baked throughout the night, making fifty trays of bars until the other bakers arrived to start their shift. In the meantime, I worked with our sales crew to cut and pack the bars on large catering trays for each location. I made sure we loaded the trays into the truck in the order we would need for the delivery and mapped out our route. We had at least thirty large catering trays to be delivered at 10 a.m. sharp. We used the old Toyota Land Cruiser that Sam and I share with my parents.

Then I was off with a crew of three, two employees and a friend, to SoHo to deliver the goodies. We double-parked, dealt with building security, freight elevators, and receptionists at each location. It was a frenzy, but in the end, by about 10:20 a.m., it was over without a hitch. Though exhausted, we felt proud and victorious. To this day when we are considering taking a catering order, we always say, "If we can deliver four thousand mini bars to SoHo by 10 a.m., we can do anything."

Southern Cherry Chess Bars

Makes 12 bars or 24 mini bars

Nonstick cooking spray

1/2 cup (1 stick) unsalted butter

1 (15- to 16-ounce) package
    yellow cake mix

1 large egg

1 cup canned cherry pie filling

Cheesecake Filling (page 110)

1/3 cup sifted confectioners' sugar

Heat the oven to 350°F. Line a 9-by-13-inch baking pan with aluminum foil, allowing enough foil to overlap the edges. Spray the foil with cooking spray. Melt the butter in a small saucepan over low heat or in a glass bowl in the microwave. Let cool. Empty the cake mix into a large bowl. Add the melted butter and egg and mix with a wooden spoon until a dough forms. Spread the dough into the prepared pan. Dollop the cherry pie filling evenly onto the dough. Spread on the Cheesecake Filling and smooth the top. Bake until deep brown and puffy, 35 to 45 minutes. Cool completely in the pan. The cake will fall as it cools. Using a sifter, dust with confectioners' sugar. Grab the foil handles with both hands, and lift the bars out of the baking pan. Cut into 12 or 24 bars.

Fruit and Cheese Bars

Makes 12 bars

Nonstick cooking spray

Shortbread Crust (page 102)

Streusel Topping (page 81)

½ cup old-fashioned oats (not quick-cooking)

1 (15-ounce) can chopped canned peaches, drained, then dried in a dishtowel

1 cup fresh raspberries, rinsed and gently dried in a dishtowel

½ cup semisweet chocolate chips

Cheesecake Filling (page 110)

Heat the oven to 350°F. Line a 9-by-13-inch baking pan with aluminum foil, allowing enough foil to overlap the edges. Spray the foil with cooking spray. Place the Shortbread Crust into the prepared baking pan, making sure to distribute evenly. Press down on the crumbs to form a crust. Bake until golden brown, about 15 minutes. While the crust is baking, combine Streusel Topping with the oats in a small bowl. Fold the peaches, raspberries, and chocolate chips into the Cheesecake Filling in a medium bowl. When the crust is done, take it out of the oven and immediately spread the fruit mixture carefully over the top. Sprinkle the oat streusel evenly over the fruit. Return the pan to the oven and bake until golden brown, another 18 to 20 minutes. Cool completely in the pan. Grab the foil handles with both hands, and lift the bars out of the baking pan. Cut into 12 bars.

Connecting with Our Customers

Not a day goes by that Darren and I do not get a chance to meet Pauley's "biggest" fan. All of them. Her fans travel from far and wide to visit the shop and everyone at Donna Bell's really shows them how thankful we are for their visits. We have had people from all over the world fly to New York and come straight to the bake shop from the airport. And there are times when the perfect opportunity arises to surprise Pauley's fans and have them say hello to her when she happens to be on the phone. It's a fun way to keep her connected to the shop and her fans when she is busy out in Los Angeles.

Besides her fans, we get lots of customers who are from the South. They always seem surprised when I mention that I am from Pittsburgh, especially when they taste my soups, or home-made drop biscuits. But I just explain that in Pittsburgh, like in the South, we love our portions big, and our food rustic and comforting. Once we had an attorney come into the shop and order some chicken and dumplings. As she sat in our little window seat and ate, she started to cry. She said that she grew up in Georgia and her mother had passed several years ago and that she thought she would never again taste chicken and dumplings like her mother had made. In those moments, I am proud of my family and what they were able to pass on to me. I'm humbled that Pauley trusted and believed in me. It's hard to explain, but I like to make my food taste like home. I wish my grandparents were around to see what I have done, especially since they were my greatest inspiration and so supportive of everything I did while growing up. They would have really enjoyed this and I would have been so honored to share it with them.

LEFT: *Matthew hosting a field trip for local city kids, January 2014.*
ABOVE: *Michael Weatherly visiting the shop.*

Friends and Family Make It Work

Part 4

Donna Bell in Our Hearts

From the very beginning, it was important to all three of us to set the right mood for the shop. We wanted to express the warmth of a real Southern kitchen, so we put mementos from my mother on the walls. My mother loved to paint. Her small painting of a bowl of daisies (that I remember from my childhood home) hangs on one wall. One of her handwritten recipes, framed, hangs on another.

Recently, Matthew called, very excited, to tell me that he had found new wallpaper for the shop. He sent me a picture and I couldn't believe it: It was the wallpaper I fell in love with when I was twelve years old. It looked just like the designer wallpaper my mom and I found in a clearance rack, something we never would have bought, but thanks to a hefty discount could afford. My room, with those little tiny roses all over the walls, was the most beautiful thing and made me feel like such a lucky girl. When I saw the tiny flowers on Matthew's wallpaper, I cried. It's so warm, so happy, and reminds me of my little childhood bedroom.

One of the most touching things for me about the bakery is the "spirit of Donna Bell" that fills the shop. Darren and Matthew have both said they want to honor her memory in not only the decor and the food, but in the way we make people feel. They are committed to treating people with kindness and grace just like she would. Because her name is on our door, we want you to be greeted with her spirit immediately when you walk in. Being a part of the shop's ideology keeps her memory alive in our hearts.

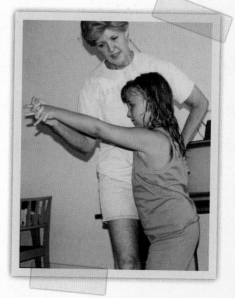

OPPOSITE: *Donna Bell with Pauley and her sister Andi at the lake.* RIGHT: *Donna Bell dancing with her granddaughter and Pauley's niece, Lauren.*

Peanut Butter Bars

Makes 12 bars or 24 mini bars

Nonstick cooking spray

2¼ cups (4½ sticks) unsalted butter, divided

3 cups (one 28-ounce jar) creamy peanut butter

3 cups sifted confectioners' sugar

Oat Crust (page 114)

1½ cups semisweet chocolate chips

Heat the oven to 350°F. Line a 9-by-13-inch baking pan with aluminum foil, allowing enough foil to overlap the edges. Spray the foil with cooking spray. Melt 1½ cups of the butter in a large saucepan over low heat. When the butter is completely melted, take the pan off the heat, add the peanut butter, and whisk until smooth. Add the confectioners' sugar, 1 cup at a time, whisking until smooth. Set aside. Place the Oat Crust into the prepared baking pan, making sure to distribute evenly. Press down on the crumbs to form a crust. Bake for 5 minutes. Remove the crust from the oven and immediately pour the peanut butter filling over the crust. Cover and refrigerate for 45 minutes. In a small saucepan, melt the remaining ¾ cup butter over low heat. When the butter is completely melted, take the pan off the heat and add the chocolate chips. Beat with an electric mixer until smooth. Pour the chocolate sauce over the chilled peanut butter filling, and spread evenly over the top. Cover and refrigerate for another 30 minutes. Grab the foil handles with both hands, and lift the bars out of the baking pan. Cut into 12 or 24 bars.

When Pauley Visits

Pauley doesn't get to New York City as much as she used to but it is always exciting when she does, and having her in the shop is great fun. Typically we hear at least once a day: "Is Abby here?" "Is Pauley in today?" Or my favorite, the simple "Is she in?"—to which I say, "Yes, Pauley is doing dishes in the back . . . just kidding." Everyone gets a good laugh and before their disappointment takes over, I win them back with the offer of a rice crispy treat or our renowned peanut butter bar. But to see the faces of her fans when they walk in *and* actually see Pauley behind the counter wearing a DBBS apron is the best. There are gasps, laughs, hugs, and photos. Pauley is wonderful with her fans.

One would think that when a best friend moves across the country that distance would hurt your relationship. But the exact opposite occurred for us. Pauley and I have become closer since she moved to L.A. When Pauley and I get together it's all about quality time, not quantity. One of our favorite things to do is to just sit for hours, catching up. She says her favorite place to sit in New York City is on the small balcony of my apartment.

Now that we've created Donna Bell's, we have another place to meet and spend time together. When Pauley comes to the shop she finds me at the counter and Matthew in the kitchen whipping up something delicious. All of our worlds merge in that one *tiny* place. The space is covered with wallpaper that Pauley had when she was a little girl, covered with pictures of all of us and, of course, Donna. It has Donna's painting of daisies from the '70s. It is truly a space filled with heirlooms and love. Sometimes we will sit in the window seats after we've closed and talk and laugh until our stomachs hurt. We all appreciate this precious time together because life is so busy these days.

ABOVE: *Pauley and goddaughter, Olive, at Darren and Sam's wedding, 2014.*

Keeping My Thanksgiving Tradition Going

After moving back to New York, in the back of my mind I kept wondering how I could celebrate my favorite holiday. In Los Angeles I had a huge house with lots of room for guests. My tiny one-bedroom walk-up in Hell's Kitchen just didn't feel like the place to pull off something this important. Then one day it just came to me: "I should have dinner at the shop." I invited everyone I knew, including my family from Pittsburgh, Darren's family from the city, the Donna Bell's crew, their families, and even some of our customers and neighbors who had no plans for dinner that day. Our shop is small, but I rented tables, chairs, dishes, chafing pans, and even champagne flutes. Thanksgiving is our busiest time of the year, so after baking hundreds and hundreds of pies and desserts, I then went right into roasting turkeys, folding napkins, chilling wine, and cooking the dozens of side dishes that come with an Uncle Matthew Thanksgiving dinner.

We closed the shop and all of our dinner guests were able to walk over from the Macy's Thanksgiving Day Parade only two blocks away. Everyone squeezed into the shop and feasted. It was funny when passers-by on the street saw fifty people crammed into our tiny lobby eating dinner. A few German tourists even asked for a reservation. We now do Thanksgiving at the shop every year, and not only does it get easier, but it's growing. There is something very special about having Thanksgiving in New York City, but also having dinner in the shop you own, blocks from Times Square, surrounded by family and friends, that makes it completely perfect.

ABOVE: *Family, friends, and staff all enjoying Thanksgiving dinner at our small shop.* LEFT: *Matthew's folks at Thanksgiving in New York City at Donna Bell's.*

Cranberry White Chocolate Rice Krispies Treats

Makes 12 treats

Nonstick cooking spray

1/4 cup (1/2 stick) unsalted butter

2 (10-ounce) bags mini marshmallows, divided

6 cups Rice Krispies

1/2 cup dried cranberries

1/2 cup white chocolate chips

1/2 recipe Vanilla Sauce (page 33), optional

Line a 9-by-13-inch baking pan with aluminum foil, allowing enough foil to overlap the edges. Spray the foil with cooking spray. Melt the butter in a stockpot over low heat. When melted, add 1½ bags of the marshmallows. Still over low heat, stir until smooth. Remove from the heat and add the cereal, cranberries, and remaining ½ bag of marshmallows. Mix to combine. Add the white chocolate chips. Quickly mix together and scrape the mixture into the prepared pan. Spray your hands with cooking spray and press firmly until even. Let cool for 1 hour. Drizzle with Vanilla Sauce if you like. Grab the foil handles with both hands, and lift the treats out of the baking pan. Cut into 12 squares.

Blueberry Cheesecake Crunch Bars

Makes 12 bars or 24 mini bars

Nonstick cooking spray

Shortbread Crust (page 102)

Streusel Topping (page 81)

½ cup old-fashioned oats (not quick-cooking)

2 cups fresh blueberries, stems removed, rinsed and dried in a dishtowel

Cheesecake Filling (page 110)

Heat the oven to 350°F. Line a 9-by-13-inch baking pan with aluminum foil, allowing enough foil to overlap the edges. Spray the foil with cooking spray. Place the Shortbread Crust into the prepared baking pan, making sure to distribute evenly. Press down on the crumbs to form a crust. Bake until golden brown, 15 to 18 minutes. While the crust is baking, combine the Streusel Topping with the oats. Fold the blueberries into the Cheesecake Filling. Take the crust out of the oven and immediately spread the blueberry filling carefully over the top. Sprinkle the oat streusel over the filling. Return to the oven and bake until Streusel Topping is golden brown, another 18 to 20 minutes. Cool completely in the pan. Grab the foil handles with both hands, and lift the bars out of the baking pan. Cut into 12 or 24 bars.

Hanging Out at the Shop

Most of my time is spent in Los Angeles because of my job. When I travel to New York, I am always there for some kind of work event. I am usually doing a talk show or a press function. I stay in the area close to the shop so I can be with the boys and the Greenblatts if I have any downtime.

My life is completely different when I'm in Manhattan now, as opposed to when I lived there years ago. Fame changes every aspect of your life. I'm not very comfortable with it and never aspired to be famous, so the change has been very hard for me. Gone are the days when I could just walk or skate around without a care. The paparazzi can be more difficult in New York than in Los Angeles, because in L.A. you are often in your car; in New York, you are usually out on the street. It's the beauty of New York that there are people walking around all the time, but if you're being sought by paparazzi, it leaves you far more vulnerable. I also feel a responsibility to my fans to look at least halfway decent when I go out in public because I don't want their pictures with me to be awful. That can sometimes be a lot for someone who would stay in her pajamas all day long if it were her choice.

It's for all these reasons that I never announce when I'm going to be at the bake shop. I just go in, put on an apron, and get behind the counter. I love being there and I feel like I'm back to a normal life, just behind the counter with my friends making people happy with our delicious treats. Even though there are pictures of me all over the shop, many people don't realize it's actually me behind the counter. They just don't expect me to be there wearing an apron. When people do recognize me, it's always really funny. They don't believe it at first and then we take fun pictures.

One of my very favorite things to do is to take goodies down the street to the FDNY Engine 54 fire station. My cousins, uncle, and dad are all firefighters, so I feel like I'm with family when I make this visit. We pack up cupcakes and cookies, walk down to the station, and surprise the firefighters—and almost always end up taking pictures with them. These heroes, who are like celebrities to me, always greet me and treat me with such warmth; I am always delighted to spend time with them. After all, I've been hanging out in firehouses my whole life—it feels like home visiting them.

OPPOSITE and ABOVE: Pauley visiting the local firehouse.

Chocolate Chip Cookies

Makes 12 cookies

1 cup (2 sticks) unsalted
butter, softened

1 cup packed light brown
sugar

1/2 cup granulated sugar

2 large eggs

1 teaspoon vanilla extract

3 cups all-purpose flour

1 teaspoon baking powder

1/4 teaspoon baking soda

2 cups semisweet chocolate
chips

In a large bowl, beat the butter and brown and granulated sugars together with an electric mixer on medium speed. On low speed, add the eggs, one at a time, mixing well after each addition. Scrape the bowl. Add the vanilla and mix again. In another bowl, whisk together the flour, baking powder, and baking soda. Add one-third of the flour mixture to the wet ingredients, mixing slowly on low speed. Repeat until all of the flour is incorporated. Scrape the bowl and beat on low speed for 30 seconds. Lastly, add the chocolate chips and mix until combined. Scoop the dough onto parchment paper or plastic wrap. Roll into an 8-inch log, and wrap in the paper or plastic. Refrigerate for 2 hours. Heat the oven to 400°F. Line two cookie sheets with parchment paper. Remove the dough from the refrigerator and roll it again to make sure it is round and has no flat sides, pressing the ends to ensure the log stays 8 inches long. Cut the log in half. Wrap one log in plastic wrap and return it to the refrigerator. Cut the other half into 6 equal slices. Place them on one of the prepared cookie sheets, making sure to leave about 1 inch between cookies. Bake for 5 minutes. Turn the oven temperature down to 325°F, and bake until lightly browned, an additional 10 to 15 minutes. Let cool completely on the cookie sheet. While the first batch is cooling, increase the temperature to 400°F, and follow the same directions for the second log.

Getting Behind Talent and Creativity

Darren

Matthew's culinary talent helps drive the success of the shop. It is a pleasure to see him flourish on a daily basis and to help him realize his vision for Donna Bell's. Matthew wasn't formally trained as a cook or baker but he singlehandedly created every recipe that we use at the shop. Donna inspired the atmosphere and the food, but it is Matthew's tasty temptations that our customers love so much.

Now that he has perfected our "basics," Matthew can experiment with different ingredients and create new variations. I am constantly amazed how his food vocabulary and palate have developed over the years and I am very proud of his culinary talent.

We have a small and extremely talented team that feels like a family. Matthew and I may have different management styles but we both have a strong appreciation for how hard our employees work. Matthew is really funny, always telling stories and making everyone laugh. He likes to cook for the crew and has a generous spirit. I am more serious and less whimsical but the crew knows they can talk to me about anything with no judgments and I will have their back. Our managerial approach is one of caring, empathy, and support—it's what makes the shop work.

Learning to Make the Best of Every Situation

Matthew

It's now a few years into our business and we are adapting to all the curve balls constantly thrown our way. We've learned from our mistakes (we've made quite a few), and we absolutely use our insights and projections to make life a little simpler. One of Darren's quotes is "Think smarter, not harder." Our little crew has also become more amazing than I ever could have imagined. We laugh sometimes, thinking back to our beginnings and the little things that we thought were so difficult then. "Remember when we only used to make two trays of biscuits?" I'll ask. It felt like such a triumph to do so and now we make at least twenty every day.

Some things will never change, though. We still shop locally for almost everything we use at the shop. There is a farmers' market a few blocks away that we visit daily. Making use of any spare time, while driving to wholesale stores in the Bronx, we will conduct impromptu business meetings right there inside our rental van. If the crew is needed to work overtime, I like to supplement their extra pay with a nice home-cooked meal to show my appreciation. The best part is that we are always closed on Sundays. It's awesome to know that the staff has this permanent day that they can spend with their families, get away from the city, go to the park or to church; it's a guaranteed day of rest. So in the middle of all the craziness that is New York City, it's nice to know that Donna Bell's is a place where you can feel relaxed like you are at home. It's all about setting the mood. I always try to stay positive, not worry about the little things, and enjoy what I've worked so hard for.

Turtle Cupcakes

Makes 18 cupcakes

1½ cups all-purpose flour

¾ cup unsweetened cocoa powder

1 teaspoon baking soda

½ teaspoon kosher salt

½ cup buttermilk

½ cup brewed coffee, at room temperature

¾ cup (1½ sticks) unsalted butter, softened and divided

1 cup granulated sugar

½ cup packed light brown sugar

2 large eggs

2 teaspoons vanilla extract

1 cup chopped pecans

Homemade Caramel Sauce (page 29), warm

½ cup semisweet chocolate chips

Heat the oven to 375°F. Line two 12-cup muffin tins with cupcake liners. In a small bowl, whisk together the flour, cocoa powder, baking soda, and salt. Mix the buttermilk and coffee together in a small pitcher. In a large bowl, beat ½ cup of the butter with the granulated and brown sugars together with an electric mixer on medium speed until light and fluffy. Add the eggs, one at a time, beating well after each addition. Mix in the vanilla. Add the flour mixture alternately with the buttermilk mixture, beating well after each addition and scraping the bowl at least once. Fill the prepared cups two-thirds full. Bake until a toothpick inserted in the centers comes out clean, 15 to 20 minutes. Cool completely and remove from the pans. Add the pecans to the warm Homemade Caramel Sauce. Spoon over the cupcakes. Microwave the remaining ¼ cup butter in a small bowl for 1 minute to melt. Add the chocolate chips and stir until the chips are melted and the mixture is smooth. Drizzle over the finished cupcakes.

Strawberry Shortcake with Fresh Whipped Cream

Serves 8 to 16

Nonstick cooking spray

4½ cups all-purpose flour

3 cups granulated sugar

4½ teaspoons baking powder

1 teaspoon baking soda

2 teaspoons kosher salt

1 cup (2 sticks) unsalted butter, softened and cut in pieces

2 cups whole milk

½ cup sour cream

1 Tablespoon vanilla extract

3 large eggs

2 large egg yolks

Fresh Whipped Cream (page 146)

3 cups sliced fresh strawberries, or 1 cup sliced fresh strawberries, 1 cup fresh blueberries, and 1 cup fresh raspberries

Heat the oven to 350°F. Spray three 9-inch round cake pans with cooking spray. Cut rounds of parchment paper to fit the pans, place in the pans, and spray the parchment with cooking spray. In a large mixing bowl, whisk together the flour, sugar, baking powder, baking soda, and salt. Add the butter, milk, sour cream, and vanilla. Beat with an electric mixer on medium speed for 5 minutes, stopping occasionally to scrape the sides of the bowl. Add the eggs and egg yolks, one at a time, beating after each addition. Beat for 3 more minutes at medium speed. Pour the batter into the prepared cake pans, dividing equally. Smooth the tops. Bake until firm to the touch and a toothpick inserted in the centers comes out clean, 30 to 35 minutes. Let the cakes cool in the pans for 5 minutes. Remove from the pans and transfer to wire racks to cool completely. Place one cake layer on a serving plate. Place one-third of the Fresh Whipped Cream in the center of the cake, then spread it out over the top and slightly over the sides of the cake. Layer with one-third of the strawberry slices and other berry mix, if using. Repeat with the second and third layers.

Butter Pecan Cake with Buttercream Frosting

Serves 8 to 16

Nonstick cooking spray
1½ cups (3 sticks) salted butter
½ cup sour cream
½ cup whole milk
2 teaspoons vanilla extract
4 cups all-purpose flour
2 teaspoons baking powder
2½ cups granulated sugar
5 large eggs
3 cups chopped pecans, toasted, divided
Buttercream Frosting (page 146)

Heat the oven to 350°F. Spray three 9-inch round cake pans with cooking spray. Cut rounds of parchment paper to fit the pans, place in the pans, and spray the parchment with cooking spray. In a medium skillet, melt the butter over medium-low heat until brown. Cook, stirring occasionally, until the butter foams, has a rich brown color, and the bottom of the pan is speckled with browned bits of the milk solids, 8 to 10 minutes. Watch carefully so it doesn't burn. Pour the butter into a large mixing bowl and let cool. In a small bowl, whisk together the sour cream, milk, and vanilla. In a separate bowl, whisk together the flour and baking powder. Add the sugar to the butter and beat with an electric mixer on medium speed until smooth. Add the eggs, one at a time, beating well after each addition. Add the flour mixture alternately with the sour cream mixture, beating well after each addition. Fold in 2 cups of the pecans. Divide the batter evenly among the prepared pans. Smooth the tops, and bake until firm to the touch and a toothpick inserted in the centers comes out clean, 30 to 35 minutes. Let cakes cool in pans for 5 minutes. Remove from the pans and transfer to wire racks to cool completely. Mix ¾ cup of the remaining pecans

Butter Pecan Cake with Buttercream Frosting *(cont.)*

into the Buttercream Frosting. Place one cake layer on a serving plate. Place one-quarter of the buttercream in the center of the cake, and spread it out to the edges. Repeat with the second and third layers. Frost sides with remaining buttercream. Sprinkle remaining ¼ cup pecans on top for garnish.

Buttercream Frosting

2 cups (4 sticks) unsalted butter, softened

2 teaspoons vanilla extract

½ teaspoon kosher salt

5 cups sifted confectioners' sugar

In a large bowl, beat the butter with the paddle blade of an electric mixer on medium speed. Add the vanilla and salt and mix until smooth. Add the confectioners' sugar, one cup at a time, on low speed; beat to incorporate. Increase the speed to high, and beat until smooth after each addition. Scrape the bowl as needed.

Fresh Whipped Cream

1 quart heavy whipping cream

1 cup sifted confectioners' sugar

2 teaspoons vanilla extract

Place the cream, sugar, and vanilla in a large bowl. With an electric mixer, beat on low speed until the ingredients come together, about 30 seconds. Turn to high speed and mix until light and whipped, 2 to 3 minutes. Do not overmix.

Carrot Cake with Cream Cheese Frosting

Serves 8 to 16

Nonstick cooking spray

2 cups corn oil

2 cups granulated sugar

2 cups packed light brown sugar

5 large eggs

1 Tablespoon vanilla extract

2 teaspoons molasses

4 cups all-purpose flour

1 Tablespoon baking powder

1 teaspoon baking soda

1 Tablespoon ground cinnamon

2 teaspoons kosher salt

7 carrots, peeled and grated

1 cup golden raisins

1 cup coarsely chopped walnuts, divided, optional

Cream Cheese Frosting (page 148)

Heat the oven to 350°F. Spray three 9-inch round cake pans with cooking spray. Cut rounds of parchment paper to fit the pans, place in the pans, and spray the parchment with cooking spray. Combine the oil, granulated and brown sugars, eggs, vanilla extract, and molasses in a large bowl. Whisk until smooth. In a separate large mixing bowl, combine the flour, baking powder, baking soda, cinnamon, salt, and carrots. Mix well so the dry ingredients are incorporated and the carrots are coated with the flour mixture. Add the wet ingredients. Using an electric mixer, beat on low speed until smooth. Fold in the raisins and ¾ cup walnuts, if using. Divide the batter evenly among the prepared cake pans. Smooth the tops. Bake until firm to the touch, and a toothpick inserted in the centers comes out clean, about 45 minutes. Cool the cakes for 5 minutes in the pans. Remove from pans and transfer to wire racks to cool completely. Place one cake layer on a serving plate. Place one-quarter of the Cream Cheese Frosting in the center of the cake, and spread it out to the edges. Repeat with the second and third layers. Use remaining quarter to frost sides of cake. Sprinkle the remaining ¼ cup walnuts, if using, on top for garnish.

Cream Cheese Frosting

1 cup (2 sticks) unsalted butter, softened

1 pound (two 8-ounce packages) cream cheese, softened

2 teaspoons fresh lemon juice

1 teaspoon vanilla extract

½ teaspoon kosher salt

6 cups sifted confectioners' sugar

Place the butter and cream cheese in a large bowl, and beat together with an electric mixer on medium speed until smooth. Add the lemon juice, vanilla, and salt. Mix again until smooth. Add the confectioners' sugar, 1 cup at a time, on low speed; beat to incorporate. Then increase the speed to high, and beat until smooth after each addition. Scrape the bowl as needed.

The Sound Track of Our Lives

I often think of music when I think of Pauley and Matthew. Music has always played a large part in Pauley's life. She sang in church as a little girl, recorded albums solo and with bands, and now meets her music idols at the Grammys each year as a correspondent for CBS. When you are with Pauley, there's rarely a time that music isn't playing. Once while we were traveling from Atlanta to Alabama to see her parents, we stopped at a truck stop and bought a Dolly Parton cassette. Pauley sang every song on that cassette, instantly turning me into a Dolly fan.

Matthew has eclectic taste. I can tell what kind of mood he is in when I step into the shop in the morning. Sometimes it's Madonna Mondays, or he's singing show tunes, or even playing old episodes of *The Golden Girls* on his computer. Our customers often walk out humming "Thank You for Being a Friend"! But my favorite music at the shop is Matthew's country mix. It started off with about twenty songs but he kept adding so now there's about eight hours of old and new country music. I think our customers appreciate being transported to a different place when they step in our front door. One told us, after hearing it play at the shop, that he had kissed his first girl back in 1980 while listening to "Sunday Morning Coming Down" by Kris Kristofferson. Proof that music (and food) can be powerful tools that transport us back in time and spark memories of important events in our lives.

Matthew and I had known each other for a long time, but over the past four years we have become a family, sometimes dysfunctional like any family, but a family just the same. I know wherever we go from here we will always have the incredible shared experience of Donna Bell's Bake Shop. And I'm positive that whenever I hear "Harper Valley P.T.A." by Jeannie C. Riley, I will be right back behind the counter of Donna Bell's, making people happy through baked goods.

Champagne Cake with Strawberry Buttercream Frosting

Serves 8 to 16

Nonstick cooking spray

4 cups all-purpose flour

4 teaspoons baking powder

1 teaspoon kosher salt

1½ cups (3 sticks) unsalted butter

3 cups granulated sugar

½ cup sour cream

1 teaspoon vanilla extract

1 large egg

7 large egg whites

2 cups Brut champagne

Buttercream Frosting (page 146)

10 fresh strawberries

Heat the oven to 350°F. Spray three 9-inch round cake pans with cooking spray. Cut rounds of parchment paper to fit the pans, place in the pans, and spray the parchment with cooking spray. In a large bowl, whisk together the flour, baking powder, and salt. Set aside. In a large mixing bowl, beat the butter and sugar with an electric mixer on medium speed for 1 minute. Increase speed to high and beat until light and fluffy, about 4 more minutes. Add the sour cream and vanilla and beat to combine. Add the whole egg and egg whites, one at a time, beating after each addition. On low speed, beat in the flour mixture alternately with the champagne, one-third at a time, starting with the flour and ending with the champagne. Beat to combine after each addition. Divide the batter evenly among the prepared pans. Smooth the tops. Bake until a knife inserted in the centers comes out clean, about 35 minutes. Let the cakes cool in the pans for 5 minutes. Remove from the pans and transfer to wire racks to cool completely. Finely chop 6 of the strawberries and stir into the Buttercream Frosting. Mix well. Place one cake layer on a serving plate. Place one-quarter of the buttercream in the center of the cake, and then spread it out to the edges. Repeat with the second and third layers. Frost the sides with the remaining buttercream. Slice the remaining 4 strawberries in half and use to garnish the cake.

Looking to the Future

We have a ten-year lease for Donna Bell's retail space. Ideally, I suppose we will try to keep the shop open for as many years as we possibly can. Realistically, you hear horror stories of how many businesses in the city shut down after their leases expire, due to the extraordinary rent increases. That's life in New York City. So far we haven't really talked about what we will do when that time comes.

Running just one small bake shop is quite a challenge and it seems daunting to think of a franchise. But we always hear, "You need a Donna Bell's in (fill in the blank)" from our customers. Though I've settled into life here in New York, I have no way of knowing where my love of adventure will take me years from now.

The most obvious decision we could make right now would be to open a Donna Bell's Kitchen somewhere close in the neighborhood. Opening a second shop would be much easier than the first time around. All of those mistakes we made would never be repeated, the red tape of New York City wouldn't be so intimidating, and we already have a very loyal customer base. My friends back in Los Angeles also remind me often: "We are still waiting for a Donna Bell's out here," and my family in Pittsburgh tells me, "If you ever want to open a shop here let us know; we would love to help." There are so many options. I guess all I have to do is open shops everywhere and I could spend the rest of my life traveling between all the places. All too easy, huh. Or as we say in the baking business, "a piece of cake."

OPPOSITE: Still baking as gifts. Wedding cake and treats for Matthew's cousin Kat.

Coconut Custard Pie

Serves 8

Nonstick cooking spray

1/2 recipe Shortbread Crust
  (page 102)

1/4 cup (1/2 stick) unsalted
  butter

6 large eggs

1 1/2 cups granulated sugar

1 cup whole milk

1 cup sweetened cream of coconut

2 teaspoons vanilla extract

2 teaspoons coconut extract

4 cups sweetened flaked coconut

1/4 cup all-purpose flour

1 teaspoon kosher salt

Heat the oven to 350°F. Spray a 9-inch springform pan with cooking spray. Place the Shortbread Crust into the prepared pan, making sure to distribute evenly. Press the crumbs firmly onto the bottom and 1 inch up the side of the pan to form a crust. Melt the butter in a small saucepan over low heat or in a glass bowl in the microwave. Let cool. In a large bowl, whisk together the eggs and sugar. Add the cooled melted butter, milk, cream of coconut, vanilla, and coconut extract. Add the flaked coconut, flour, and salt. Mix completely. Pour the mixture into the crust. Cover the pan with foil and seal. Place the pan on a baking sheet and bake until the center of the pie is almost set but still somewhat jiggly, 75 to 85 minutes. Remove the foil and bake until the pie is golden brown and firm to the touch in the center, an additional 10 to 15 minutes. For safety, check that the internal temperature is 160°F to ensure the eggs are cooked. Cool for 5 minutes. Unlatch and remove the sides of the springform pan. Let the pie cool for another 30 minutes. Chill, covered, in the refrigerator overnight.

A Sweet Ending

From an idea inspired by my mom, three friends accomplished a dream and opened Donna Bell's Bake Shop. It's funny and touching to look back on the history of how we all came together to create this place. The shop has brought so much joy to so many people. Whether it's a passer-by who knows nothing about the shop and just stops in, or a fan who has traveled from another country to visit Donna Bell's, they get a small taste of our vision. Stepping in from the busy sidewalks and streets of New York City to the warmth of our kitchen and shop is like visiting a little oasis.

Though the three of us come from different backgrounds, we are lucky that the strangeness of life brought us together. Our collective experiences created a perfect partnership for this endeavor: We have a bake shop we are proud of and excited to share with the world. We hope you have enjoyed our stories, maybe had a laugh or a tear, learned about what it's like to start a company, and most important, enjoyed the food. Come in and see us sometime. We'd love to feed you!

ABOVE: *Donna Bell's storefront — December 2014.*

Acknowledgments

Very special thanks to:

Sandra and Dennis L. Sandusky, Audrey and Irwin Greenblatt, Samuel Hunt, Andi, Aunt Vicki Milner, Ryan Greenblatt, Katie Barker, Kristen Hall, Paula Jacobson, Sheilah Kaufman, Christopher Glawe, Lisa Wisely, James McKenny, Ali Smith, Joshua Bright, Heather A. Stillufsen and Rose Hill Designs, Jeremy Murphy, Kareem Elgohary, Joey Fuller, to our extremely hardworking and talented crew, and to our customers, who make every day worth it.

Index

A

allspice

Pumpkin Spice, 81

almonds

Cinnamon Almond Cranberry Coffee Cake, 46–7

apples

Granny Smith apples

Apple Sausage Muffins, 36–7

pie filling

Apple-Filled Sweet Biscuits with Homemade Caramel
Sauce, 26–8

apricots

Dried Fruit Scones with Lemon Glaze, 65

B

Bacon Blue Cheese Parsley Biscuits, 16–7

bananas

Banana Pecan Muffins, 72–3

Banana Scones with Orange Glaze, 60

bars

Blueberry Cheesecake Crunch Bars, 132–3

Cheddar Jalapeño Corn Bread Squares, 92–3

Cranberry White Chocolate Rice Krispies Treats, 130–1

Frosted Brownies, 112–3

Fruit and Cheese Bars, 116, 120

Lemon Bars, 100–1

Maple Walnut Pie Bars, 104–5

Peanut Butter Bars, 126–7

Pumpkin Pie Bars, 108–9

Seasonal Magic Bars, 116–7

Southern Cherry Chess Bars, 116, 119

berries

blueberries

Blueberry Cheesecake Crunch Bars, 132–3

Blueberry-Filled Sweet Biscuits with Vanilla Sauce, 24–5

Sweet Lemon Corn Bread Muffins with Fresh Blueberries, 96–8

Strawberry Shortcake with Fresh Whipped Cream, 142–3

cranberries

Cinnamon Almond Cranberry Coffee Cake, 46–7

Cranberry Orange Spice Bread Pudding with Orange Glaze, 90–1

Cranberry White Chocolate Rice Krispies Treats, 130–1

Dried Fruit Scones with Lemon Glaze, 65

Seasonal Magic Bars, 116–7

raspberries

Fruit and Cheese Bars, 116, 120

Strawberry Shortcake with Fresh Whipped Cream, 142–3

strawberries

Champagne Cake with Strawberry Buttercream Frosting, 150–1

Strawberry Scones with Lemon Glaze, 50–1

Strawberry Shortcake with Fresh Whipped Cream, 142–3

biscuits

Apple-Filled Sweet Biscuits with Homemade Caramel Sauce, 26–8

Bacon Blue Cheese Parsley Biscuits, 16–7

Blueberry-Filled Sweet Biscuits with Vanilla Sauce, 24–5

Buttermilk Biscuits, 10–1

Cheddar Pimento Biscuits, 14–5

Whole Wheat Biscuits, 20–1

blueberries

fresh

Blueberry Cheesecake Crunch Bars, 132–3

Sweet Lemon Corn Bread Muffins with Fresh Blueberries, 96–8

Strawberry Shortcake with Fresh Whipped Cream, 142–3

pie filling

Blueberry-Filled Sweet Biscuits with Vanilla Sauce, 24–5

blue cheese

Bacon Blue Cheese Parsley Biscuits, 16–7

bread. *See also* **corn bread; French bread**

Pumpkin Chocolate Chip Loaf, 40–1

Zucchini Walnut Bread, 44–5

bread pudding

Cranberry Orange Spice Bread Pudding with Orange Glaze, 90–1

Hummingbird Bread Pudding with Cream Cheese Glaze, 86–7

brownies

Frosted Brownies, 112–3

brut champagne

Champagne Cake with Strawberry Buttercream Frosting, 150–1

Buttercream Frosting

Butter Pecan Cake with Buttercream Frosting, 144–6

Champagne Cake with Strawberry Buttercream Frosting, 150–1

recipe, 146

Buttermilk Biscuits, 10–1

Butter Pecan Cake with Buttercream Frosting, 144–6

C

cake frosting

Buttercream Frosting, 146

Cream Cheese Frosting, 148

Fudge Frosting, 114

cakes. *See also* **coffee cake; cupcakes**

Butter Pecan Cake with Buttercream Frosting, 144–6

Carrot Cake with Cream Cheese Frosting, 147

Champagne Cake with Strawberry Buttercream Frosting, 150–1

Strawberry Shortcake with Fresh Whipped Cream, 142–3

Caramel Sauce

    Apple-Filled Sweet Biscuits with Homemade Caramel Sauce, 26–8

    recipe, 29

    Turtle Cupcakes, 140–1

Carrot Cake with Cream Cheese Frosting, 147

Champagne Cake with Strawberry Buttercream Frosting, 150–1

Cheddar cheese

    Cheddar Jalapeño Corn Bread Squares, 92–3

    Cheddar Pimento Biscuits, 14–5

cheese. *See also* **cream cheese**

    Bacon Blue Cheese Parsley Biscuits, 16–7

    Cheddar Jalapeño Corn Bread Squares, 92–3

    Cheddar Pimento Biscuits, 14–5

    Fruit and Cheese Bars, 116, 120

Cheesecake Filling

    Blueberry Cheesecake Crunch Bars, 132–3

    Fruit and Cheese Bars, 116, 120

    Pumpkin Pie Bars, 108–9

    recipe, 110

    Southern Cherry Chess Bars, 116, 119

cherries

    cherry pie filling

    Southern Cherry Chess Bars, 116, 119

    maraschino cherries

        Pineapple Cherry Crunch Muffins, 82–3

chocolate chips

    semisweet

        Chocolate Chip Cookies, 136–7

        Chocolate Chip Walnut Coffee Muffins, 68–9

        Frosted Brownies, 112–3

        Fruit and Cheese Bars, 116, 120

        Fudge Frosting, 114

Maple Walnut Pie Bars, 104–5

Peanut Butter Bars, 126–7

Pumpkin Chocolate Chip Loaf, 40–1

Seasonal Magic Bars, 116–7

Turtle Cupcakes, 140–1

white

Cranberry White Chocolate Rice Krispies Treats, 130–1

Seasonal Magic Bars, 116–7

cinnamon

Cinnamon Almond Cranberry Coffee Cake, 46–7

Cinnamon Scones with Maple Glaze, 61

Pumpkin Spice, 81

cocoa powder

Frosted Brownies, 112–3

Fudge Frosting, 114

Turtle Cupcakes, 140–1

coconut

Coconut Custard Pie, 154–5

Hummingbird Bread Pudding with Cream Cheese Glaze, 86–7

Maple Walnut Pie Bars, 104–5

Seasonal Magic Bars, 116–7

coffee

brewed

Turtle Cupcakes, 140–1

instant

Chocolate Chip Walnut Coffee Muffins, 68–9

coffee cake

Cinnamon Almond Cranberry Coffee Cake, 46–7

cookies. See also bars; squares

Chocolate Chip Cookies, 136–7

corn, creamed

Cheddar Jalapeño Corn Bread Squares, 92–3

corn bread

    Cheddar Jalapeño Corn Bread Squares, 92–3

    Sweet Lemon Corn Bread Muffins with Fresh Blueberries,
        96–8

cranberries

    dried

        Cinnamon Almond Cranberry Coffee Cake, 46–7

        Cranberry White Chocolate Rice Krispies Treats, 130–1

        Dried Fruit Scones with Lemon Glaze, 65

        Seasonal Magic Bars, 116–7

    fresh or frozen

        Cranberry Orange Spice Bread Pudding with Orange
            Glaze, 90–1

cream cheese

    Cheesecake Filling, 110

    Cream Cheese Frosting, 148

    Cream Cheese Glaze, 33

Cream Cheese Frosting

    Carrot Cake with Cream Cheese Frosting, 147

    recipe, 148

Cream Cheese Glaze

    Hummingbird Bread Pudding with Cream Cheese Glaze,
        86–7

    recipe, 33

creamed corn

    Cheddar Jalapeño Corn Bread Squares, 92–3

crumb topping. *See* **Streusel Topping**

crunch bars

    Blueberry Cheesecake Crunch Bars, 132–3

crusts

    Oat Crust

        Frosted Brownies, 112–3

        Peanut Butter Bars, 126–7

recipe, 114

Shortbread Crust

Apple-Filled Sweet Biscuits with Homemade Caramel
Sauce, 26–8

Blueberry Cheesecake Crunch Bars, 132–3

Blueberry-Filled Sweet Biscuits with Vanilla Sauce, 24–5

Fruit and Cheese Bars, 116, 120

Coconut Custard Pie, 154–5

Lemon Bars, 100–1

Pumpkin Pie Bars, 108–9

recipe, 102

Seasonal Magic Bars, 116–7

cupcakes. *See also* **cakes**

Turtle Cupcakes, 140–1

Custard Pie, Coconut, 154–5

D

dates

Dried Fruit Scones with Lemon Glaze, 65

dried apricots

Dried Fruit Scones with Lemon Glaze, 65

dried cranberries

Cinnamon Almond Cranberry Coffee Cake, 46–7

Cranberry White Chocolate Rice Krispies Treats, 130–1

Dried Fruit Scones with Lemon Glaze, 65

Seasonal Magic Bars, 116–7

dried dates

Dried Fruit Scones with Lemon Glaze, 65

Dried Fruit Scones with Lemon Glaze, 65

F

filling

Cheesecake Filling, 110

for pies, canned

    Apple-Filled Sweet Biscuits with Homemade Caramel
        Sauce, 26–8

    Blueberry-Filled Sweet Biscuits with Vanilla Sauce, 24–5

    Southern Cherry Chess Bars, 116, 119

French bread

    Cranberry Orange Spice Bread Pudding with Orange Glaze,
        90–1

    Hummingbird Bread Pudding with Cream Cheese Glaze, 86–7

Fresh Whipped Cream

    recipe, 146

    Strawberry Shortcake with Fresh Whipped Cream, 142–3

Frosted Brownies, 112–3

frosting

    Buttercream Frosting, 146

    Cream Cheese Frosting, 148

    Fudge Frosting, 114

fruit

    apples

        Apple-Filled Sweet Biscuits with Homemade Caramel
            Sauce, 26–8

        Apple Sausage Muffins, 36–7

    apricots

        Dried Fruit Scones with Lemon Glaze, 65

    bananas

        Banana Pecan Muffins, 72–3

        Banana Scones with Orange Glaze, 60

    blueberries

        Blueberry Cheesecake Crunch Bars, 132–3

        Blueberry-Filled Sweet Biscuits with Vanilla Sauce, 24–5

        Sweet Lemon Corn Bread Muffins with Fresh Blueberries,
            96–8

        Strawberry Shortcake with Fresh Whipped Cream, 142–3

cherries
    Pineapple Cherry Crunch Muffins, 82–3
    Southern Cherry Chess Bars, 116, 119
cranberries
    Cinnamon Almond Cranberry Coffee Cake, 46–7
    Cranberry Orange Spice Bread Pudding with Orange
        Glaze, 90–1
    Cranberry White Chocolate Rice Krispies Treats, 130–1
    Dried Fruit Scones with Lemon Glaze, 65
    Seasonal Magic Bars, 116–7
dates
    Dried Fruit Scones with Lemon Glaze, 65
peaches
    Fruit and Cheese Bars, 116, 120
    Peach Muffin Streusel, 80
pineapple, canned crushed
    Hummingbird Bread Pudding with Cream Cheese Glaze,
        86–7
    Pineapple Cherry Crunch Muffins, 82–3
pumpkin puree
    Pumpkin Chocolate Chip Loaf, 40–1
    Pumpkin Pie Bars, 108–9
raisins
    Carrot Cake with Cream Cheese Frosting, 147
    Dried Fruit Scones with Lemon Glaze, 65
raspberries
    Fruit and Cheese Bars, 116, 120
    Strawberry Shortcake with Fresh Whipped Cream, 142–3
strawberries
    Champagne Cake with Strawberry Buttercream Frosting,
        150–1
    Strawberry Scones with Lemon Glaze, 50–1
    Strawberry Shortcake with Fresh Whipped Cream, 142–3

Fudge Frosting

Frosted Brownies, 112–3

recipe, 114

G

ginger

Pumpkin Spice, 81

glazes. *See also* **sauces**

Cream Cheese Glaze, 33

Lemon Glaze, 33

Maple Glaze, 35

Orange Glaze, 35

golden raisins

Carrot Cake with Cream Cheese Frosting, 147

Gorgonzola cheese

Bacon Blue Cheese Parsley Biscuits, 16–7

Granny Smith apples

Apple Sausage Muffins, 36–7

H

Homemade Caramel Sauce, 29

honey

Caramel Sauce, 29

Maple Walnut Pie Bars, 104–5

Hummingbird Bread Pudding with Cream Cheese Glaze, 86–7

I

icing. *See* **frosting; glazes; sauces**

instant coffee

Chocolate Chip Walnut Coffee Muffins, 68–9

Italian sweet sausage

Apple Sausage Muffins, 36–7

J

jalapeño peppers

Cheddar Jalapeño Corn Bread Squares, 92–3

L

Lemon Bars, 100–1

Lemon Glaze

Dried Fruit Scones with Lemon Glaze, 65

recipe, 33

Strawberry Scones with Lemon Glaze, 50–1

Sweet Lemon Corn Bread Muffins with Fresh Blueberries, 96–8

loaves

Pumpkin Chocolate Chip Loaf, 40–1

M

Magic Bars, Seasonal, 116–7

Maple Glaze

Cinnamon Scones with Maple Glaze, 61

recipe, 35

maple syrup

Maple Glaze, 35

Maple Walnut Pie Bars, 104–5

maraschino cherries

Pineapple Cherry Crunch Muffins, 82–3

marshmallows

Cranberry White Chocolate Rice Krispies Treats, 130–1

molasses

Carrot Cake with Cream Cheese Frosting, 147

Pumpkin Chocolate Chip Loaf, 40–1

muffins

Apple Sausage Muffins, 36–7

Banana Pecan Muffins, 72–3

Chocolate Chip Walnut Coffee Muffins, 68–9

Peach Muffin Streusel, 80

Pineapple Cherry Crunch Muffins, 82–3

Sweet Lemon Corn Bread Muffins with Fresh Blueberries, 96–8

N

nutmeg

Pumpkin Spice, 81

nuts

almonds

Cinnamon Almond Cranberry Coffee Cake, 46–7

pecans

Banana Pecan Muffins, 72–3

Butter Pecan Cake with Buttercream Frosting, 144–6

Hummingbird Bread Pudding with Cream Cheese Glaze,
86–7

Seasonal Magic Bars, 116–7

Turtle Cupcakes, 140–1

walnuts

Carrot Cake with Cream Cheese Frosting, 147

Chocolate Chip Walnut Coffee Muffins, 68–9

Maple Walnut Pie Bars, 104–5

Zucchini Walnut Bread, 44–5

O

Oat Crust

Frosted Brownies, 112–3

Peanut Butter Bars, 126–7

recipe, 114

oats

Blueberry Cheesecake Crunch Bars, 132–3

Fruit and Cheese Bars, 116, 120

Oat Crust, 114

Pumpkin Pie Bars, 108–9

Orange Glaze

Banana Scones with Orange Glaze, 60

Cranberry Orange Spice Bread Pudding with Orange Glaze,
90–1

recipe, 35

orange juice

Cranberry Orange Spice Bread Pudding with Orange Glaze,
90–1

Orange Glaze, 35

P

parsley

Bacon Blue Cheese Parsley Biscuits, 16–7

peaches

Fruit and Cheese Bars, 116, 120

Peach Muffin Streusel, 80

Peanut Butter Bars, 126–7

pecans

Banana Pecan Muffins, 72–3

Butter Pecan Cake with Buttercream Frosting, 144–6

Hummingbird Bread Pudding with Cream Cheese Glaze,
86–7

Seasonal Magic Bars, 116–7

Turtle Cupcakes, 140–1

pie bars

Maple Walnut Pie Bars, 104–5

Pumpkin Pie Bars, 108–9

pie filling, canned

Apple-Filled Sweet Biscuits with Homemade Caramel Sauce,
26–8

Blueberry-Filled Sweet Biscuits with Vanilla Sauce, 24–5

Southern Cherry Chess Bars, 116, 119

pies

Coconut Custard Pie, 154–5

pimento

Cheddar Pimento Biscuits, 14–5

pineapple, canned crushed

Hummingbird Bread Pudding with Cream Cheese Glaze, 86–7

Pineapple Cherry Crunch Muffins, 82–3

preserves

Strawberry Scones with Lemon Glaze, 50–1

pudding, bread. *See* **bread pudding**

pumpkin puree

Pumpkin Chocolate Chip Loaf, 40–1

Pumpkin Pie Bars, 108–9

Pumpkin Spice

Cranberry Orange Spice Bread Pudding with Orange Glaze, 90–1

Peach Muffin Streusel, 80

Pumpkin Chocolate Chip Loaf, 40–1

Pumpkin Pie Bars, 108–9

recipe, 81

R

raisins

Carrot Cake with Cream Cheese Frosting, 147

Dried Fruit Scones with Lemon Glaze, 65

raspberries

Fruit and Cheese Bars, 116, 120

Strawberry Shortcake with Fresh Whipped Cream, 142–3

Reese's Pieces

Seasonal Magic Bars, 116–7

Rice Krispies

Cranberry White Chocolate Rice Krispies Treats, 130–1

S

sauces. *See also* **glazes**

    Caramel Sauce, 29

    Vanilla Sauce, 33

sausage

    Apple Sausage Muffins, 36–7

scones

    Banana Scones with Orange Glaze, 60

    Cinnamon Scones with Maple Glaze, 61

    Dried Fruit Scones with Lemon Glaze, 65

    Strawberry Scones with Lemon Glaze, 50–1

Seasonal Magic Bars, 116–7

semisweet chocolate chips

    Chocolate Chip Cookies, 136–7

    Chocolate Chip Walnut Coffee Muffins, 68–9

    Frosted Brownies, 112–3

    Fruit and Cheese Bars, 116, 120

    Fudge Frosting, 114

    Maple Walnut Pie Bars, 104–5

    Peanut Butter Bars, 126–7

    Pumpkin Chocolate Chip Loaf, 40–1

    Seasonal Magic Bars, 116–7

    Turtle Cupcakes, 140–1

Shortbread Crust

    Apple-Filled Sweet Biscuits with Homemade Caramel Sauce, 26–8

    Blueberry Cheesecake Crunch Bars, 132–3

    Blueberry-Filled Sweet Biscuits with Vanilla Sauce, 24–5

    Fruit and Cheese Bars, 116, 120

    Coconut Custard Pie, 154–5

    Lemon Bars, 100–1

    Pumpkin Pie Bars, 108–9

    recipe, 102

Seasonal Magic Bars, 116–7

shortcake

Strawberry Shortcake with Fresh Whipped Cream, 142–3

Southern Cherry Chess Bars, 116, 119

spice

Pumpkin Spice, 81

squares. *See also* **bars**

Cheddar Jalapeño Corn Bread Squares, 92–3

Cranberry White Chocolate Rice Krispies Treats, 130–1

Frosted Brownies, 112–3

strawberries

fresh

Champagne Cake with Strawberry Buttercream Frosting, 150–1

Strawberry Scones with Lemon Glaze, 50–1

Strawberry Shortcake with Fresh Whipped Cream, 142–3

preserves

Strawberry Scones with Lemon Glaze, 50–1

Streusel Topping

Blueberry Cheesecake Crunch Bars, 132–3

Cinnamon Almond Cranberry Coffee Cake, 46–7

Fruit and Cheese Bars, 116, 120

Peach Muffin Streusel, 80

Pumpkin Pie Bars, 108–9

recipe, 81

Sweet Lemon Corn Bread Muffins with Fresh Blueberries, 96–8

T

topping. *See* **Streusel Topping**

treats. *See also* **bars**

Cranberry White Chocolate Rice Krispies Treats, 130–1

Turtle Cupcakes, 140–1

V

Vanilla Sauce

Blueberry-Filled Sweet Biscuits with Vanilla Sauce, 24–5
Cranberry White Chocolate Rice Krispies Treats, 130–1
recipe, 33

W

walnuts

Carrot Cake with Cream Cheese Frosting, 147
Chocolate Chip Walnut Coffee Muffins, 68–9
Maple Walnut Pie Bars, 104–5
Zucchini Walnut Bread, 44–5

Whipped Cream

recipe, 146
Strawberry Shortcake with Fresh Whipped Cream, 142–3

white chocolate chips

Cranberry White Chocolate Rice Krispies Treats, 130–1
Seasonal Magic Bars, 116–7

Whole Wheat Biscuits, 20–1

Y

yellow cake mix

Southern Cherry Chess Bars, 116, 119

Z

Zucchini Walnut Bread, 44–5

About the Authors

Pauley Perrette is one of the top Q-rated actors in television and film and is currently playing Abby on the number one TV show *NCIS*. She is also a producer, director, philanthropist, activist, songwriter, singer, and writer. Pauley was raised all over the South but considers Alabama her home state. She currently lives in Los Angeles.

Darren Greenblatt was a creative entrepreneur in the fashion industry for over twenty years. Darren's exquisite talent for design and entrepreneurial spirit, coupled with being a lifelong foodie, was the spark that started Donna Bell's Bake Shop.

Matthew Sandusky is co-owner and head baker for Donna Bell's Bake Shop. Matthew's experience working in the food industry for many years and his natural talent for baking has helped Donna Bell's flourish.